THE LITTLE BOOK OF COUNTY WEXFORD

THE LITTLE BOOK OF COUNTY WEXFORD

NICKY ROSSITER

This book is for Anne,
Mark, David, Kate, Paula,
Ellie, Finn, Lola, Ziggy, Jack, Jude and Noah

First published 2014

The History Press Ireland
50 City Quay
Dublin 2
Ireland
www.thehistorypress.ie

© Nicky Rossiter, 2014

The right of Nicky Rossiter to be identified as the Author
of this work has been asserted in accordance with the
Copyrights, Designs and Patents Act 1988.

All rights reserved. No part of this book may be reprinted
or reproduced or utilised in any form or by any electronic,
mechanical or other means, now known or hereafter invented,
including photocopying and recording, or in any information
storage or retrieval system, without the permission in writing
from the Publishers.

British Library Cataloguing in Publication Data.
A catalogue record for this book is available from the British Library.

ISBN 978 1 84588 840 4

Typesetting and origination by The History Press

CONTENTS

	Introduction	7
1.	County Wexford	8
2.	Places	15
3.	People	42
4.	Events	59
5.	The Great War	69
6.	Ireland's Own	72
7.	Crime	75
8.	Musical County	88
9.	Working Wexford	97
10.	County Wexford and the Sea	104
11.	Religion	115
12.	Looking Back	121
13.	Miscellany	125
	Bibliography	142

INTRODUCTION

Welcome to *The Little Book of County Wexford*. As with its predecessor, it is not a formal history or chronicle of the 'Model County' but rather a collection of interesting, intriguing and often previously unpublished bits and pieces.

While researching history books we come across hundreds of gems of local information that are not strictly relevant to the projects at hand. Thanks to the computer, we can store and catalogue these for future use. These can be articles about obscure people or events. They can also turn out to be wonderful little pieces of information that are too small to make an article but much too valuable to discard.

This is where the 'Little Book' comes into its own. Here is an opportunity for the writer to share those 'I bet you never knew' or 'you will not believe this' nuggets with the reader that make the lives of our ancestors just that bit more real, such as the first aeroplane in New Ross, a little-recalled murder and a priest founding a town called Wexford in America. We are not concerned with the big historical figures, unless it is to explode some little myth like Michael Collins and the Pierce bicycles.

In quotes from older texts the original spellings are maintained. Reading the words aloud can often give a hint of their current meaning.

1
COUNTY WEXFORD

To set the scene, here is a brief overview of County Wexford. According to the 2011 census the population of the county was 145,320, while in 1982 it stood at 99,016. The estimated population in 1841 was 202,033, having grown from 170,806 in twenty years. The Great Famine had much less of an effect on the number of people in the county than in other areas, with the figure dropping to 180,158 in 1851. In the following seventy-five years there was a steady decrease until there were only 95,848 recorded in 1926.

The land area is 908.5 square miles. For those who like statistics, Wexford is the thirteenth largest of Ireland's thirty-two counties in area and fourteenth largest in terms of current population. It is the largest of Leinster's twelve counties in size. It is bounded by the sea on two sides: to the south by the Atlantic Ocean and to the east by St George's Channel and the Irish Sea. The River Barrow forms its western boundary and the Blackstairs Mountains form part of the boundary to the north as do part of the Wicklow Mountains.

Like other counties, there are a number of divisions of land. Baronies are parts of a county or a group of civil parishes and may span parts of more than one county. Their origin is thought to date from Norman or pre-Norman times and may be based on the Gaelic family territories. This division was used from the sixteenth to the nineteenth century in surveys, land transactions and censuses. Wexford has the baronies of Gorey, Scarawalsh, Ballaghkeen North, Ballaghkeen South, Bantry, Shelmaliere West, Shelmaliere East, Shelburne, Bargy and Forth. There are 2,384 townlands in the county so we will not list them here, and there are also parish divisions.

In the sixteenth century the south of County Wexford had families like the Devereuxes (incidentally pronounced Dever-X in Wexford rather than the French-sounding Dever-O), Brownes and Staffords, while the north of the county was predominantly Gaelic with Kinsellas, O'Murroughs (Murphys) and the MacMurrough-Kavanaghs.

More prominent later planters were the Colcloughs (pronounced Coakly) in the 1550s, the Mastersons in the 1560s and Sir Henry Wallop who acquired lands at Enniscorthy in the early 1580s. By 1600, settlers like Wallop owned 35 per cent of the land in the barony of Scarawalsh. In 1606 north Wexford was officially 'shired' and divided into the baronies of Ballaghkeen, Scarawalsh and Gorey.

The census of 1659 and the poll tax roll of 1660 showed that 11.9 per cent of County Wexford's population was 'New English'. Despite this, of five Wexford MPs in the 1660 Convention, four were Cromwellian soldiers or adventurers, showing the power of this new elite.

Between 1700 and 1735 the major exports from County Wexford were beef (at 47 per cent), along with wheat, barley and oats. By 1760 beef exports accounted for 63 per cent with butter the second major export while grain made up a mere 2 per cent. The value of exports from Wexford had fallen by almost a fifth while Irish exports in general had increased. Almost all grain was being shipped through Dublin. In 1757 there were attempts to stop the shipping of all grain out of the county because of large-scale crop failure and fears of another famine like that of 1740/41, when several hundred thousand died in Ireland.

The situation changed in a few years with the Irish Parliament's campaign leading to a massive increase in grain exports from Wexford after 1782. Most went to Britain but there was also a significant export to Spain. New Ross was a busy port with over half of its barley and wheat going to Portugal and Spain between 1791 and 1816. It was the main point of departure for provisions to Newfoundland – where County Wexford fishermen had settled in the eighteenth century having followed the fishing trade there.

Much has been written of the 1798 rebellion so we will content our narrative with some of the causes and consequences.

The Militia Act of 1793 sought to create local armed corps under the control of magistrates from the landowning class. It was made up of recruits selected at random from the local population using a ballot system rather than volunteers, making it most unpopular. There was a clash between the Wexford Militia under Captain Boyd and a large crowd who attempted to rescue some prisoners in July 1793 and it was reported that dozens of people were killed.

In addition to the militia, there were also around 1,000 yeomanry in the county. Orangeism was strong within the yeomanry; outside Ulster, the Orange Order was probably strongest in Wexford of all parts of Ireland as a consequence of 1798 and it grew in strength in the 1830s. The yeomanry was highly unpopular nationally since 1798 and a crucial event in their demise took place at Newtownbarry in June 1831. They were called out to deal with a protest over the sale of cattle that had been seized for non-payment of tithes. They attacked the protesters and killed at least twelve. Following this and other incidents nationally, the yeomanry began to be replaced by the constabulary. By 1834 there were thirty-four constabulary barracks with a total of 218 men stationed in County Wexford.

Potato blight first appeared in County Wexford in September 1845. The county was not one of the worst areas affected but it did suffer during the Famine. Maize, also known as Indian meal, was imported in an effort to provide relief (on 26 January 1847, *Niobe*, carrying maize from New York, was wrecked on the Keeragh Islands) but complaints that the relief was inadequate came from New Ross in 1846 and then from Enniscorthy and Wexford in 1847. In July 1848 the Wexford Board proposed that the absentee landlords meet any shortfalls in money for relief. Protests over lack of work and food broke out in 1846, resulting in Wexford having the thirteenth heaviest constabulary presence in the country. Wexford, coincidentally, had the thirteenth highest rate of eviction in the decade immediately after the Famine. The county also had the highest emigration rate of any Leinster county, apart from Dublin, after 1850.

In October 1880 a branch of the Land League was founded at Barntown, County Wexford. Among the tactics it employed was the disruption of foxhunts, and this led to the suspension of the Wexford Hunt in January 1882.

Land and labour associations for farm labourers existed in Wexford from the 1880s. Workers in other areas also began to organise themselves and the National Union of Sailors and Firemen was organised in the county in the 1890s. The firemen in question were not firefighters but those employed to tend the boilers on steam ships.

In Easter 1916 the Wexford Volunteers occupied the Athenaeum in Enniscorthy for five days. The county inspector claimed that large numbers of armed civilians had volunteered their assistance against the republicans. Among the arrests in 1916 were 270 County Wexford people. Of these, 150 were interned at Frongoch in North Wales. It was said that, because so many GAA members from both Wexford and Dublin were at Frongoch, that the two counties played the 1916 Leinster football final there. Nine Wexford men were court-martialled and six sentenced to death, but the sentences were all commuted.

Family businesses were established and grew in County Wexford throughout the late nineteenth and early twentieth centuries. Pierce's agricultural implements and Star Engineering were the main businesses in Wexford town. Davis Flour Mills, Roche's Malting, Buttle's Bacon and Donohoe's Mineral Water gave employment in Enniscorthy. Farming continued to be an important element of Wexford's economic life and the National Farmers' Association was established in the county in the 1950s. Staffords imported coal through both Wexford and New Ross's and the Albatross Fertiliser Company was established in New Ross in the 1940s.

WEXFORD TOWNS

The principal towns of the county are Wexford, Enniscorthy, New Ross and Gorey.

County Wexford

Wexford (*Loch Garman*) was founded by the Vikings around AD 800. They named it Veisafjord (inlet of the mud flats) and the name has changed only slightly into its present form. For about 300 years it was a Viking town; largely independent and owing only token dues to the Irish Kings of Leinster. In 1653, following the Cromwellian campaign, the town (with 6,000 acres) was offered for sale by the English Parliament for £5,000. There were no bidders.

Enniscorthy (*Inis Córthaidh*) is the second-largest town. The origins of the town's name may refer either to the 'Island of Corthaidh' or the 'Island of Rocks'. Dating back to AD 465, Enniscorthy is one of the longest continuously occupied sites in Ireland. The Norman castle, rebuilt in 1586, now houses the County Museum. In 1798 Enniscorthy became a focus of the rebellion when, after a month of bloody fighting, the Irish rebels were defeated at the Battle of Vinegar Hill which stands above the town of Enniscorthy.

New Ross (*Ros Mhic Thriúin*) is located on the River Barrow, near the border with County Kilkenny and is the third-largest town in the county in terms of population, with around 8,000 residents. The earliest settlement in this area is Irishtown, which dates back to the fourth century, when St Abban founded a monastery there. In about the sixth century it was still comprised of a monastery and school. Following the arrival of the Normans in 1169, New Ross achieved a major strategic importance. In oral tradition it is said that trades such as drapers, butchers and wainwrights were required to give one day's labour each week to assist in constructing the town walls. On Sundays it was said to be the time for the women to help and they constructed 'Lady's Gate', which later became 'Three Bullet Gate'. The new title recalls the year 1649, when Cromwell's forces fired three cannon rounds at the gate before the town surrendered.

Gorey (*Guaire*) is a market town in the north of the county. It claims existence from the nucleus of a town dating back to 1296.

Wexford's county nickname is the Model County. It is said to be derived from its progressive farming methods and model farms. The first agricultural school in Ireland was opened in Wexford in the 1850s, although the nickname 'Model County' was already used in 1847.

2

PLACES

When we open a book about a place like County Wexford, our first focus is on the many places that combine to make up the larger entity. In our exploration of County Wexford we will pick a few places at random to give the reader a flavour, not only of the county as we know it but also its wider influence.

ANOTHER WEXFORD

Just after the Famine, a priest called Thomas Hoare (Hore) is said to have led a group of about 1,000 people, principally from the south Wicklow and north Wexford area, to settle eventually in Little Rock, Arkansas. This would have been at the invitation of the bishop of that area, Andrew Byrne.

Hoare and his people initially travelled from Ireland to Liverpool. There they are reported to have chartered three ships, *Ticonderoga*, *Loodianah* and *Chasca*. Despite the chartering of such vessels, conditions were as bad as on any famine or coffin ship. Bad food, poor sanitation, seasickness and overcrowding made the journey horrific.

Father Hoare, in *Ticonderoga*, reached New Orleans after forty days at sea. The *Loodianah* arrived a full seventeen days later. During the perilous voyage, *Chasca* was blown off course – this was a common occurrence in such times – and ended up in the Virgin Islands seeking provisions. They spent Christmas on the islands and finally arrived at New Orleans ten weeks after leaving Liverpool.

As was to be expected, not all the travellers continued on their journey. About 470 had travelled on the ship with Hoare and some, tired of travelling, decided to settle in New Orleans. Others struck out for Refugio in Texas, where a number of people from their home area in Ireland had settled two decades earlier. The remainder continued to Little Rock.

On arrival they found that all was not as expected. The bishop's representative had died and they were left without food, jobs or even shelter. The conditions were awful and within days cholera broke out. Twenty of their number perished, including Mary Breen aged 13 years. Disillusioned, only eight families decided to try to make a home in Little Rock. Others headed for Saint Louis and Father Hoare led others to Fort Smith on the edge of Native American territory. He later went to Saint Louis and appears to have convinced about eighteen families to move with him to Iowa and on to the lands of the Winnebago tribe. There they settled and founded a town they called Wexford.

Here we come upon two versions of what happened next. In one version, Father Hoare remained with the new settlement for four or five years but, owing to ill health or advancing age, he felt it necessary to resign his pastoral duties. After getting permission from his bishop in Dubuque, he went to a Trappist monastery in a place called New Mellary and made an offer to the abbot. In exchange for sending a priest and some brothers to Wexford to minister to the flock, he offered the lands and houses to the monastery. This was agreed and Father Francis Walsh and five lay brothers proceeded to the Wexford colony. In 1885 they are said to have returned to their monastery and the abbot sold the land to neighbouring farmers. The colony survived and, in 1870, the original log church built by Father Hore was replaced by a stone edifice.

Records in Ireland appear to contradict this. These show that Father Hore returned to Ireland in 1851, just a few months after settling his flock in Iowa. He was appointed curate at Caim and later to Cloughbawn. The good priest died on 14 June 1864 and was buried at Cloughbawn.

BARONY OF FORTH

According to Amyas Griffith, writing in July 1764, Carns Oard – probably Carnsore – was situated south of Wexford town. It consisted of about 60 acres of land, of which many were 'stony and unprofitable'. In that area lived six large families who among them had 36 horses, 18 cows, 104 sheep and some pigs and geese, and who sent barrels of barley and beans to market.

Griffith reported that people of the area rose at four o'clock in summer and worked until noon. Then they ate a hearty meal and slept until two o'clock before continuing to work until six o'clock. Then they returned home to 'make merry with families' and retire at eight o'clock to bed. The females were said to be famed for their beauty and all had a sprightly turn of wit and raillery. Disobedience to parents was said to be a 'never forgiven' crime. There is said to be great hospitality, with houses open to strangers and no locks on 'doors, chests or cupboards'.

The giant Phelim Nathahana was said to be buried there, in a grave 23ft long, and some claimed to have seen his rib bone that was 6ft in length.

Marriage: Males in the Barony of Forth general married at the age of 18 to 20 years, with females marrying between 14 and 16 years of age. Weddings were a major occasion. First a large malthouse or barn was cleared and tables and benches (plus bales of straw) were placed around it. Then the whole population of the townland attended.

Griffith reported that the happy couple were 'joined by the priest's hands' and an oaten ring was placed on the bride's finger. The bride was then 'smacked by every person present' after a collection had been taken up to pay the priest. They also collected for the piper and for the 'itinerant beggars' who had assembled to celebrate with the happy couple.

The guests then seated themselves for the meal. The bride had pride of place at the head of the tables with the priest at the opposite end and bridesmaids and bridesmen arranged in order. The bridegroom acted as servant and 'does not presume to sit at table'. All but the bride and groom could eat and drink heartily.

After the nuptial feast, the bride was be lifted over the table by the chief bridesman to give the first dance. An apple was thrown in the air and the man who caught it had his choice of bridesmaid as a dance partner. After the dancing, the bridesmen formed a party and abducted the bride. A hue and cry was raised as the groom led a posse in pursuit. This was said to test his true love in pursing his bride.

Death: On the occasion of a death, according to Griffith, the whole neighbourhood went in silent procession. There was no howling or keening, as in other parts of Ireland, and 'they do not pay women to screech and make Indian-like noises over their relatives'. The direct family of the deceased neither feast, shave nor 'make merry' for six weeks.

Writing in 1780, Vallency recorded that the men of the area wore short coats and trunk breeches, with a round hat and narrow trim. The women favoured a short jacket and petticoats bordered at the bottom with one to three bands of different colours. All were said to be of good morals. He noted that the poorest farmers had meat twice a week with the wealthier ones feasting daily on beef, mutton or fowl. All drank home-brewed ale and beer. The women were said to undertake all labour except ploughing and to receive equal wages with the men. The primary fuel was furze 'grown on the tops of dykes'.

SEVENTEENTH-CENTURY COUNTY WEXFORD

In the summer of 1634 Sir William Brereton visited County Wexford. He and his companions, Plummer and Needham, are said to have been on the lookout for investment opportunities.

Places 19

That summer was reported as warm, with much of the pastureland scorched. There were further references to great woodland areas and much trade in timber. Enniscorthy was stated to have more merchants involved in timber products than any other. Coopers and 'dish turners' were numerous and every house had wooden trenchers (wooden plate), dishes, bowls, noggins (small drinking cups), pails, tubs and casks.

Wool and flax weaving were common small industries. At Clohamon the group witnessed lime being burnt to enrich the soil.

They were entertained at Clonmullen by Morgan Kavanagh, who they described as 'an honest fair dealing man' and 'his lady' a good woman. They noted, however, that both were recusants (those refusing to conform to the Established Church). They were given good beer, sack and claret and noted that, in dispensing this, the host was 'no nigard'. Kavanagh's wife Eileen is said to have been the inspiration for the song 'Eileen Aroon'. The family would lose their lands in the Cromwellian plantations a few decades later.

In Enniscorthy they lodged at the house of Andrew Plummer on 16 July, paying a shilling each for themselves and sixpence for their servants. In that town they spent £2 4s on a 'little white mare' before crossing the Slaney by horse and heading for Carrig, where the river was crossed via 'a narrow ferry'. In this area they 'found divers [lots] of the Roches'.

A nearby farm called 'The Parke' was leased by an Englishman named Hardey with his landlord being William Synode of The Lough. They thought his farm almost an island, with water on three sides.

Reaching Wexford, they lodged at 'the sign of the Windmill' in the house of Paul Bennett. In Wexford they noted trade in the harbour was much decayed and poor due to the failure of the

herring fishery. In times past it was said that half a dozen men could land £20 to £40 worth of herring in a single night's fishing. On their inspection, Brereton and his companions found the town impoverished and the quays in disrepair.

At the Wexford Assizes, Sir George Shirley, Lord Chief Justice of Ireland, presided over *nisi prius* cases (these were a sort of pre-trial hearing). Sir John Philpot, judge of common pleas, adjudicated cases of misdemeanours and 'trials of life and death'. A local Justice of the Peace warned the travellers of rebels abroad in the countryside armed with 'pieces, pistols, darts and skenes'. They witnessed one such rebel being led to his execution at the castle. They recalled women and others following the prisoner and 'making lamentations as if they were distracted' and indulging in a kind of 'tone singing'.

Of the general population they noted that 'most of the women are clear skinned and bare necked with a crucifix tied in a black necklace between their breasts'. They also stated that there were many papists in the town who were unashamed of their religion. In fact, the mayor Mark Cheevers and the Sheriff of the Shire accompanied the judges to their church door but then left to attend Mass 'which is tolerated and publicly resorted to in three or four houses'. The attendance at the Protestant service was small. The mayor's fare did not impress the writers who referred to a wife who 'could not carve, cook, entertain or demean herself'. He was served 'charter beer, mighty, thick and muddy, which he did not taste'.

THE ISLAND

Our Lady's Island is situated about 10 miles from Wexford. It lies on Lough Togher (Lake of the Causeway a salt-water lake), separated from the wild Atlantic by a sandbar at Carnsore Point. To people of the county 'The Island' usually denotes the locality.

This island is one of the oldest shrines to Our Lady in Ireland and tradition tells us that it has been a place of pilgrimage since the earliest days of Christianity. There is a belief that the island was actually without its current causeway in ancient times and as such may have attracted the attention of the early Celtic monks who often repaired to secluded places for prayer and contemplation. The monks of St Abban are associated with the island in folklore. The association of the feast of the Assumption with this pilgrimage site also lends credence to the early origin of the shrine. It is one of the four oldest feasts associated with Our Lady and the first recorded mention dates to St Gregory of Tours in the sixth century. Located close to Ptolemy's 'Sacred Cape' (often identified as Carnsore), there is a distinct possibility that the whole area was a place of pagan worship and, therefore, Our Lady's Island may have been one of the many such locations converted to Christian pilgrimage by the Celtic monks.

The first recorded pilgrimages to Our Lady's Island date from the early Normans.

There was a castle built on the island around 1237 by the de Lamporte family, but they later handed this over to the Canons Regular of St Augustine. This may have happened because of the existing popularity of the island as a place of pilgrimage. Between the twelfth and seventeenth centuries, the Canons Regular of St Augustine had charge of two celebrated places of pilgrimage: these were Lough Derg and Our Lady's Island and both were linked. The season at Lough Derg began on 1 June and continued until 15 August. Pilgrims then made their way to Our Lady's Island where the pilgrimage continued until 8 September.

In 1607 Pope Paul V granted indulgences to 'places of piety and pilgrimage' in Ireland and these included St Patrick's Purgatory and Our Lady's Island. It is said in folklore that the church on Our Lady's Island was 'built with the offerings of infirm pilgrims'. Father Synnott wrote in 1670 about pilgrims 'making some oblation or extending charitable benevolence to indigents there residing have been miraculously cured of grievous maladies and helped to use naturally defected limbs or accidentally enfeebled or impared [*sic*] senses'.

Writing in 1684, Colonel Solomon Richards states:

> In this Barony of Forth is a lough called Lough Togher and in this lough is an island called Lady's Island, in former times of

> ignorance highly esteemed and accounted holy. To this day the natives in abundance from remote parts of the kingdom do with great devotion go on their pilgrimage thither and there do penance going bare foot and bare legged dabbling in the water up to mid leg round the island. Some great sinners go on their knees in the water around the island and some others that are greater sinners go three time round on their knees.

He also notes tales of people leaving 'hose and shies in Wexford and go bare foot in dirty weather from Wexford to the island'.

Local tradition maintains that while Lough Derg escaped prohibition under the 1702 statute of Queen Anne, Our Lady's Island may also have been saved from this. It cites the fact that a Barony of Forth deputation managed to secure immunity of South Wexford from plantation and extrapolates that this could also have saved the pilgrimage site.

In the eighteenth century, Our Lady's Island and Lough Derg were the only two places of pilgrimage to be exempted from the suppression imposed on other holy sites by Pope Benedict XIV because of alleged abuses.

In 1887 a boy named Cogley was searching for eels in the mud in a shallow part of the water near Our Lady's Island. He pulled up what appeared be a metal figure with one arm missing. He brought it to Archdeacon Roche, who was parish priest of Our Lady's Island and an authority on local history and traditions. Roche recalled a folk tale that told how, when Cromwell was besieging Wexford town in 1649, some of his troops went through South Wexford looting and burning the churches. The people of St Ibar's, hearing of their approach, rushed to the church. Over the tabernacle stood a silver crucifix and they took this away for safekeeping. A boy named Duffy is said to have been taking it to safety across the shallow portion of the lake when he was shot. The relic found by the boy was that of the long-lost figure of this old crucifix of St Ibar's.

A report in the *Wexford People* newspaper in 1897 notes 'The people of the parish remember pilgrims from distant places coming to the island before the Great Famine of 1847 and making circuit on their bare knees ... some old people recall seeing pilgrims from Kilkenny and elsewhere coming here in strange cloaks and taking their food with them to do their rounds.' Interestingly, it has another piece about an altar and statue being erected 'at a spot where some school children had an exciting experience of a mysterious character some years ago'.

In 1954, designated the Marian Year, the famous Irish American priest Father Peyton included Our Lady's Island in his 'crusading visit' to Ireland. Known as 'the rosary priest', he attracted an estimated 40,000 people to the pilgrimage site in one of his many 'family rosary rallies'. Hundreds of people camped out overnight on the island and, on the day itself, the authorities estimated that up to 300 cars passed through Killinick every ten minutes – remember that this was 1954 when cars were less common.

Our Lady's Island continues to be a popular site of pilgrimage from 15 August to 8 September each year, with thousands of people attending each day and coach-loads of people from the parishes of the diocese making special pilgrimages on days set aside for their locality.

JOHNSTOWN CASTLE

Today Johnstown Castle is a favourite destination for locals and tourists in need of a refreshing stroll in beautiful grounds away from the hustle and bustle of modern life.

In 1944 it was agreed that it would be donated to the Irish State to be used for agricultural research. Following an act in the Dáil in 1945, the eventual handover came in 1960. It has since been developed to incorporate not only a Department of Agriculture and Environmental Protection Agency but it also houses the Irish Agricultural Museum.

In Norman times the castle was home to the Esmondes who came to Ireland from Pembrokeshire. The first to arrive was Geoffrey de Esmonde of Huntingdon, who was one of thirty knights who landed with FitzStephen at Baginbun in 1169. The family held the lands for centuries but in 1641 they appear to have taken the wrong side in the rebellion. Oliver Cromwell's forces attacked the castle and, in 1649, and the Esmonde Estates were confiscated because of their espousal of the Catholic side in previous years.

In 1653 the townlands of Johnstown and others 'formerly the estates of Esmonde, who was implicated in the rebellion of 1641', were sent to Lieutenant Colonel John Overstreet for 'arrears of pay due to him'. Overstreet was also appointed Governor of Duncannon Fort at the time.

When Overstreet died, his widow married Edward Withers but there were no children from either marriage and in 1667, as was the normal practice in such cases, the lands were 'settled on the survivor with remainders to John Reynolds of Wexford and his wife who was niece of Bennet-Withers alias Overstreet with the remainders to their daughters Mary, Jane and Susan Reynolds'.

In 1682 John Grogan married Mary Reynolds and, on Edward's death, he came into possession of one-third of the Johnstown estate. In 1692 he purchased the other two-thirds from his sisters-in-law and from that date the Grogan family lived at Johnstown Castle. The last private resident of the castle was Lady FitzGerald who had succeeded to the estate through her mother Jane Colclough, the daughter of H.K. Grogan-Morgan.

A model of the present castle was exhibited at the Crystal Palace and it inspired Thomas Lacey to visit and to record his thoughts in his 'Home Sketches' diary in 1852. His description included, 'a splendid porch has been erected before the grand entrance' and ' on the northern side of the laboratory a handsome building was being erected, a portion of which would be appropriated to a billiard room'. Lacey noted seeing 'several herds of fine deer, followed by a number of beautiful fawns' in a deer park of 222 acres. Inside he recalled a grand hall surrounded by two magnificent galleries formed of oak with a floor 'of asphaltum, tasselated in black and white'. This led to a majestic staircase designed 'by Hopper and English architect'. The layout of the castle also included a library, estate office, gun room, school room and a ballroom. The grounds included a private graveyard.

The *Wexford Free Press* reported in 1895 that a large crowd enjoyed skating on the pond at Johnstown Castle. It went on to note that 'Workmen were engaged keeping the ice swept and at nightfall torches and flaring oil lamps were hung from the trees'.

On warm summer days and brisk autumn afternoons the once-private grounds of the castle, with its lakes, shrubs, mature

trees, walkways and statuary, attract and enchant thousands of people, young and old. There are currently plans for the interior of Johnstown Castle to be opened to the public in order to share the magnificence of this local and national treasure.

ROSSLARE HARBOUR

Rosslare Harbour can be a difficult place to write about when pinpointing its location. Many people confuse the harbour and the strand and then, to add to matters, we confuse the harbour and Ballygeary. This is probably best illustrated by the railway stations in operation: the mainland is Ballygeary and, if you continue on along the causeway, you are heading for Rosslare Harbour station; if you are up on the height above the harbour you are in Rosslare Harbour. The village is unusual for the fact that it has streets with house numbers above 1,000.

In the pre-car-ferry days, those opting to walk to the pierhead, as it was called, had to transverse a wooden walkway a few feet above the water.

The history of Rosslare Harbour dates back to the late 1870s, when work began on constructing the pier and connecting railway line.

Prior to the development, Edward Solly Flood, with George Le Hunte and others, had been a promoter of the Rosslare Railway Company and wrote a number of pamphlets extolling the superiority of conveying American mail to London via Rosslare. In his diary of 4 August 1894 he wrote: 'Drove to Wexford Station and met with Mann and Rowlands and the party who had been down at Rosslare for the opening of the line. They scolded me for not having been present, but we parted the best of friends.' This was the official re-opening of the Wexford-Rosslare Harbour Railway. The attendance of dignitaries by special train included: Hugh Maguire, Mayor of Wexford; John F. Walsh, secretary of Wexford Harbour Commissioners; John R. Cooper, solicitor, Wexford; Henry Cooper, Portland Cement Works, Drinagh; and Henry Wynne, secretary of Wexford Grand Jury. White's Hotel catered a special lunch. The first regular shipping service from Rosslare began in 1896 with a regular run to Bristol and Liverpool. Soon regular sailings began with other vessels, with services linked to railway timetables in Ireland and Britain. The two world wars brought inevitable interruptions to services out of Rosslare. During the Second World War, shipping services in and out of the port were sporadic and did not resume on a regular basis until 1946.

The actual harbour – now Rosslare Europort – was first developed in 1906 by the Great Western Railway and the Great Southern & Western Southern Railway (GS&WR) to accommodate steam-ferry traffic between Great Britain and Ireland. Although the harbour itself is located close to the previously existing settlement of Ballygeary, it was named after the village of Rosslare, some 8km away along the coast.

The GS&WR was one of the main railway operations in Ireland in the late nineteenth and early twentieth centuries. The company was the largest of Ireland's 'Big Four' railway operators, buying up smaller operations and expanding its route mileage for much of its existence.

Lifeboat Service: No busy harbour could exist without the services of the RNLI and Rosslare Harbour is no exception. In 1838 the first station to cover the area was established and the lifeboat operated from Rosslare Point at the south side of the entrance to

Wexford Harbour. This station lapsed some time after 1851 but was re-established in 1858 and was known as Rosslare Fort Station. Following the wreck of the American emigrant ship *Pomona* in 1859, with the loss of 386 people, a second larger lifeboat was stationed here in November of that year. This station was known as Wexford. In 1896 the RNLI established the Rosslare Harbour station.

Rosslare Harbour station closed in 1921, following the placing of a motor lifeboat with a permanent crew at Rosslare Point. Six years later, Rosslare Harbour station re-opened and its first motor lifeboat was kept moored to the west of the pier.

Over a period of eighty years, from 1825, two gold medals and nineteen silver medals were awarded for gallantry for saving lives off the coast.

Famously in 1914 Rosslare Harbour, Fethard, Kilmore Quay and Dunmore East lifeboats were launched to the schooner *Mexico* that had gone ashore on South Keeragh Island. The Fethard lifeboat capsized and nine of her crew of fourteen tragically drowned. Four silver medals were awarded to the crew of the Rosslare lifeboat after they rescued ten men from the schooner.

In 1929 a silver medal was awarded to Coxswain James Wickham and the bronze medal to Honorary Secretary W.J.B. Moncas for rescuing five people from the schooner *Mountblairy*.

In 1955 a silver medal was awarded to Coxswain Richard Walsh and bronze medals to Second Coxswain William Duggan and Motor Mechanic Richard Hickey when the tanker *World Concord* broke in half in hurricane-force winds on 27 November 1954. Thirty-five men were rescued by St David's lifeboat from a portion of the vessel that had drifted towards the Welsh coast. Rosslare Harbour lifeboat rescued the remaining seven men from the part that had drifted towards the Irish coast.

A bronze medal was awarded to Second Coxswain Richard Seamus McCormack for rescuing two crew from the sinking fishing boat *Notre Damedu Sacre Coeur* on 7 December 1978.

The lifeboat continues to serve seafarers in this area and to see its voluntary members most deservedly honoured for bravery.

Shipping: The Irish Continental Group story started on 17 May 1968, when the first direct Rosslare–Le Havre car ferry sailing took place. This first venture, of one round-trip sailing per week, was a joint Anglo-French operation provided by Normandy Ferries, part of P&O group, in partnership with the French shipping line Saga, owned by the Rothschild family. Both contributed a ship to the service – the *Dragon* and *Leopard*, the vessel that commenced the service. In its first season, the new service carried 31,000 passengers. In its second season, 1969, sailings were increased to two per week between mid-June and mid-August. Public reaction was enthusiastic, with the result that in 1969 passenger carryings more than doubled to 68,000. The *Dragon* and *Leopard* continued to operate during the 1970 and 1971 seasons with two sailings per week in peak season.

CIE's interest in joining Irish Continental Line stemmed from their ownership of Rosslare Harbour.

For the people of Rosslare, 31 May 1973 was a significant day. On that day, Irish Continental Line's *St Patrick* arrived for the first time, flying the Irish flag. Immediately, it began regular scheduled sailings to France, beginning with three round trips per week, increasing to every second day in each direction during July and August.

Lighthouses: The Ballast Corporation built Tuskar Rock Lighthouse in 1815. It is located on an isolated rocky islet 11km off the south-eastern corner of Ireland, marking the entrance to St George's Channel. In 1937 it had a revolving light of three faces, two of which are bright and the third deep red; and in foggy weather, the same machinery that caused the lights to revolve rings bells. It consists of a 34m-high granite tower with lantern and gallery attached to a two-storey keeper's house. The buildings are painted white. It is now classed as 'Accessible only by helicopter'. Its light continues to work and gives two quick white flashes every 7.5 seconds. There was a shore station at Rosslare, but the keeper's houses there were sold in 1973.

The Pierhead Lighthouse was built in 1906 at a station established in 1881 and located at the end of the main pier in Rosslare Harbour. The first pier light was replaced when a new pier was built in 1906. It is approximately 7.5m high and is a cast-iron tower with lantern and gallery, painted red with white trim.

LOST LANES – LOST HERITAGE

During the nineteenth and early twentieth centuries, large numbers of Wexford people lived in small houses in narrow lanes. Sadly, this heritage is being lost: the townhouses of the gentry and merchants are in varying states of preservation, but the homes of most Wexfordians have been demolished.

Mary's Lane, off Lower Bride Street in Wexford, is one of the very few to have survived. It is worth the walk just to see how people would have lived when they didn't need car parking spaces at the door. It has houses, a steep incline, a graveyard with whitewashed walls and tons of character. In fact, to walk Mary's Lane is like walking through history. From these homes you will branch right, around the graveyard and into the old malt stores, to eventually exit into an open area and then on to Peter Street. Mann's Lane branches off the lane towards Main Street. Peter Street itself was once better known as Gibson's Lane.

Across Peter Street from Mary's Lane is Foundry Lane (now called Patrick's Lane). It was named after Donnelly's Foundry. St Patrick's Fife and Drum Band spent its early days and much of the 1960s here.

Cinema Lane gained its unofficial name in 1915 when the first purpose-built cinema was opened there. It is officially called Harpur's Lane and was once Hays Lane.

Stonebridge Lane was known as 'The Hole of The Wreck' in 1910 and was inhabited at the time as a court case in 1917 refers to residents. It goes between the Sky & the Ground pub and Motor Factors. It leads, via steps, to the car park in Bride Street. In fact, that car park once contained the houses of Whetherald Court, another piece of lost heritage.

Distillery Lane was an access between the modern Devereux Villas (named after a co-owner of Wexford Distillery) and Distillery Road. Its route could still be traced on a map by coming down between Devereux Villas and St Aidan's Crescent, past Distillery House and on towards the lower end of Casa Rio.

Paradise Row can still be found with overgrown remnants of its houses. This more upmarket lane was once home to Thomas D'Arcy McGee who would rise to prominence in Canada. The lane is located between the houses of Waterloo Road (then called Methodist Row) and Corry's Villas. It leads down to the Presentation playing fields.

Slaughterhouse Lane, also known as Salthouse Lane, is still used for access. It connects lower Barrack Street to Trinity Street.

Slegg's Lane was the name of the upper portion of Keysar's Lane. It goes between Whites and FitzGerald's up to High Street. Now mainly a car park, it was once a populated area. According to the *Old Wexford Society Journal*, it was highly populated in the 1880s. In 1882 there was a kiln and warehouse advertised to let here. One of the best-known residents was Tommy Swift, the newspaper magnate.

Kaats Lane is one of the more exotically named places and yet it too is often forgotten. It would have followed the line of the present steep hill almost opposite the Vocational School. It was the location of a boat-building yard of Van Kaat in the 1600s. Before land reclamation it would have been on the riverside. Ironically, Kaats Strand, across the river, is better known.

Archers Lane ran from High Street to Main Street; it was enclosed by the old *People* newspaper offices, now Peter Mark Salon. The friars had a chapel on its north side. There was a meat market off the lane in 1880 with thirty stalls. Most of the lanes were named after the principal landowner, Clement Archer, who lived at Anne Street in 1834.

The Faythe, Ovenhouse Lane – a place where tradition has it that locals cooked their Christmas poultry – veered east, opposite Codys Lane which was near the old Swan Bar or Danny Morgans. Some traditions link this lane with Buffalo Bill Cody.

SAUNDERSCOURT

Saunderscourt once boasted an elegant Georgian mansion and an estate of about 1,000 acres stretching from the village of Crossabeg to Ferrycarrig. It owes its name to the fact that a large land grant, comprising at least 3,750 acres, was made to Colonel Robert Saunders later of the Deeps. He accompanied Oliver Cromwell to Ireland as an officer and attained the rank of colonel. In 1649, he was appointed Governor of Kinsale.

Colonel Saunders was given a residence at the Deeps, which was included in his land grant, but he apparently began construction of the mansion later known as Saunderscourt shortly after his title to the grant had been confirmed. His son Joseph is referred to as being from Saunderscourt and his grandson Richard, who died in 1730, served as MP for Wexford between 1713 and 1714. He is listed as residing at Saunderscourt.

In 1730 an indenture of marriage lists over twenty townlands in the marriage contract. It refers to land along the Slaney from the entrance to Wexford Harbour reaching up to Ballinaslaney and inland to Oulart and Oylegate. Sir Arthur Gore was created Baron Saunders of the Deeps in 1758. He died in 1773 and was succeeded by the second earl who died in 1809. It is believed that both earls are buried in the family vault in the old church ruin. Access to the vault is not now possible as the authorities sealed up the entrance to the chamber following an attempted grave robbery.

After the death of the Second Earl of Arran the family abandoned Saunderscourt and moved back to the family seat at Castle Gore in County Mayo. The mansion fell quickly into a state of disrepair as early as 1815.

The estate was purchased around 1860 by Arthur Giles who restored the mansion to its original grandeur. It was described in the writing of Thomas Lacy in 1860:

> The mansion, a fine courtly building of considerable extent, displays its rich and handsome facade, consisting of a centre and characteristic wings to the southwest. From the neat porch which stands before the centre and forms the grand entrance, the town of Wexford with its public buildings and the quay and handsome harbour, with their various vessels and small craft, came fully under observation, while the clear waters of the Slaney, spreading into a broad expanse, present the appearance of a beauteous lake in which is mirrored the umbrageous foliage that stretches along its margin.

The estate next passed into the hands of John F. Kane, who soon sold it to Crosby Harvey of Kyle in 1889 for the sum of £3,000. Captain Harvey proceeded to demolish the mansion, presumably to save on the rates.

Captain Harvey continued to farm the land until its sale in 1926 to the Land Commission.

WHITE'S HOTEL

Old White's Hotel must take some responsibility for the genetic make-up of modern Wexford. Long before there was Central Perk for Rachel and Ross, Wexford circumvented its lack of a diner or soda fountain with White's Coffee Shop.

There, on a Saturday afternoon, the young (and sometimes not so young) gathered under the watchful eye of a 'three-legged baker' in what may have been a Breugel painting, the lads congregated at their tables and the girls at theirs. In those pre-cappuccino, latte and frapaccino days, the humble black coffee was the height of sophistication.

Later that night, many of those same teenagers would troop past the coffee shop entrance, intent on admission to White's Barn. The lads would be in the aptly nicknamed 'bum freezers' – car coats for those without cars with the fake fur collar or the suede sheepskin jacket while the girls dazzled in multicoloured maxi, midi or mini dresses, whatever the weather. With the coats handed over in exchange for a cloakroom ticket it was on to face the bouncers in the hope they had not taken a dislike to you.

Inside, the lads usually headed for the balcony to the sound of the local 'relief' band – The Supreme or The Visitors – belting out their covers of the hits of the day. Down below the ladies warmed up dancing around their handbags before the crowd thickened and the serious business of 'eyeing up the talent' commenced so that serious dancing could ensue.

Later that week the evening clientele of White's Coffee Shop would have a fair sprinkling of those who had 'shifted' on the Saturday night and now most tables accommodated couples rather than groups.

LOFTUS HALL

Loftus Hall stands on the lonely promontory of The Hook. It is an impressive building with a very impressive tale told about it. Unfortunately, the tale we hear does not refer to the present building but rather the older Redmond Hall that stood on this site.

The tale dates from somewhere between 1731 and 1775 and such a wide range of years gives us doubt about its authenticity. But in any case, strange happenings are said to have haunted the resident family for years until Father Thomas Broaders was invited to lay the spirit to rest. His tomb in Horetown Cemetery is said to bear the inscription:

> Here lies the body of Thomas Broaders,
> Who did good and prayed for all
> And banished the Devil from Loftus Hall.

But what of that haunting? The story starts, as all such tales do, with a dark and stormy night and a young stranger arriving at the hall amid loud knocking. He reported having become lost in the storm and craved shelter. In line with tradition, this was granted and it appears to have become an extended stay. In those days card playing was the most common pastime and each night the stranger took part in the game with members of the family.

During one such game, Anne, the young lady of the house, dropped one of her cards. On bending to retrieve it from under the table she was shocked to see that the young stranger had a cloven hoof. She screamed and the story goes that the stranger shot through the roof in a ball of fire. Anne fainted and was carried to the tapestry room, where she hovered for weeks between life and death until she finally expired.

Local folklore maintains that the hole in the roof could never be repaired and remained until the hall was demolished in 1871. There were further tales of the hall being haunted by the stranger's spirit and of Anne's ghost being seen walking the corridors until Father Broaders exorcised it.

SOME VILLAGES AS THEY WERE IN 1885

Monamolin had a weekly fowl market every Friday and a fair day four times each year. In 1885 it boasted a population of about 100. Among the business operating in the area were: drapers run by T. Mulligan and M. Murphy; four grocers of whom two were also licensed to sell spirits; a post office with George Goff as postmaster; and a national school where Miss Clancy was the mistress.

Oulart had a population of 100, mostly farmers. There was a fowl market each Tuesday. A petty session was held every third Tuesday of the month. Moses Murphy was the postmaster.

Ballycanew in 1881 had a population of 233. It had a small tannery and a gristmill. The houses were, in general, classed as slated and in good condition. It hosted five fair days each year and a fowl market every Wednesday. A Danish fort was excavated near the village in the 1800s and burnt human remains were found in clay urns. John Miller was the Relieving Officer for the village, which also had a baker, butcher, coach builder, miller and a number of grocers. Among the landowners were families such as Bezanson, Burkitt, Furney, Gainfort, Percival and Tackaberry.

Blackwater had a population of 105 in 1881. Nearby Ballyconnigar was a favourite sea-bathing destination for Enniscorthy residents. It had a mixture of thatched and slated houses. Castle Talbot, the residence of John Talbot, was the most imposing building. Business included grocers, millers and a manure agent.

Castlebridge's population was about 400. The majority of these were farm labourers. The malt houses gave a lot of employment and a local grain market was held every day during the season.

THE STORY OF SCREEN

Screen takes its name from the old Irish word for a shrine but, ironically, it is a parish lacking in ancient remains which could explain its interesting title (according to the letters of the Ordinance Survey in the 1800s there are no known antiquities in Screen parish). In *The History of Diocese of Ferns* by Grattan-Flood (published by Downey in 1916), Screen is referred to as having been called St Nicholas' Parish in the year 1566. This is the first recorded use of the name but it possibly dates from even earlier times. Screen, which represents this old parish of St Nicholas, was dedicated to St Maelruain of Tallaght.

The Very Reverend Sylvester (Canon) Cloney was transferred to Castlebridge in April 1891 and it was he who built the present church at Screen which is dedicated to St Cyprian, a North African saint. The original church was in the townland of Garryhubbock. The present church was completed at the start of the twentieth century and has a window, dated 1901, which was dedicated by Mr Byrne of The Bullring in Wexford. The pattern day is 26 September, the feast of St Cyprian, rather than the older feast of St Nicholas. Bishop Keating refers to a dedication to Sts Cosmos and Damian whose feast is 27 September.

In the O'Donovan Letters for the Ordnance Survey in 1840, the village was noted as Skreen or as Scryn on the map. It boasted a well, 'which was nearly closed up', located 200 paces west of the site of the old church at which a pattern was held on 27 September. O'Donovan noted a holy water font in the graveyard situated on a round hillock, not unlike a moat, in the townland of Ballymore. He also noted that 'no portion of the old church remained and that there was no townland in the parish called Screen'.

Cantwell's *Memorials to the Dead* records Screen church as the chapel-of-ease of Castlebridge. He says that the graveyard remained in top condition but that the mid-nineteenth-century inscriptions were difficult to read. He may have been combining both graveyards. Among the graves recorded was: 'Richard Flynn – Chief Officer of Curracloe Coastguard Station – drowned on duty on September 8th 1868.'

Lewis' topography from around 1837 informs us that Screen lies chiefly in the barony of Ballaghkeen, located 5 miles northeast from Wexford on the coast road from Wexford to Oulart. The parish contained a total of 382 inhabitants, on land covering 977 statute acres as applotted under the tithe act. Within its limits was Ballyronan Lodge, then the property of R.S. Cuiness. The inhabitants were partly employed in the herring fishery at Curracloe. The Roman Catholic chapel was at the village of Skryne and a residence for the curate had been built on the site of the old chapel. There was also a dispensary for the poor. About sixty children were educated at a private school.

Bassett's Directory of 1885 informs us that 'this village is six miles to the north east of Wexford standing on the banks of a small trout stream known as Keating's River. There are three plantations in the area at a distance of about a quarter of a mile. The surrounding lands are suitable for tillage and pasture.'

CASTLEBRIDGE AND WEXFORD COUNTY IN 1855

The village at the time probably had a population of around 400 and, according to Lewis' 1837 topography, they lived in 'neat buildings on either side of the Castlebridge River'. By 1885, Bassett was referring to the river as the Garrylough River so in 1855 it's anybody's guess what the locals called it. If they were typical of Wexford they probably had a completely different name for it.

The fairs in Castlebridge were held on 11 April and 26 December. This latter date indicates how little Christmas holidays would have meant to a community so closely wedded to the land and its produce. The preparation of stock and produce in the days leading up to the fair impinged on the Christmas festivities, making then very low-key affairs. Fairs were popular and two more fair days were added on 10 June and 25 September. Keeping order at such fairs would have been the local constabulary with a barracks in the village.

The main business in Castlebridge was built around the corn and malting trade. Dixons established the initial business but they went bankrupt in the 1820s at which stage Breens, who were formerly excise officers, bought the malt stores. It is interesting that W.B. Nunn, the name most associated with the business, only married into the Breen family in 1875. The initials stand for William Bolton, by the way. The mill at Castlebridge was powered by water through the millrace in its early years but, by 1855, a steam engine was doing the driving.

In those years Castlebridge was a very independent village. The proximity to Wexford was almost cancelled out by the fact that you had to pay a toll – a bit like the East Link Bridge in Dublin – to go into and out of town. As you may imagine, trips were strictly limited. For business it would have been worse, as the tolls would have been levied on various items at different rates. The malt store owners got round this by using a canal from the village to the Slaney and using especially designed and built gabbards (a type of boat) to ferry the produce directly from the stores to the ships moored in Wexford Harbour.

Although the bridge owners abolished the toll in 1852, this trade by boat from Castlebridge to the ocean-going vessels survived for a further two decades. Therefore it is quite likely that the gabbards bringing the grain to the boats returned with materials for the church being constructed in those early years of the 1850s. No skipper liked to sail empty.

The man in charge of that church building was Revd Thomas Stafford, who had been appointed parish priest in April 1851. It is said that, on laying the foundation stone of the church, he picked out his own burial plot in the churchyard.

To get a flavour of what the people of Castlebridge were doing at the time of the opening of the church, we can look at the stories that appeared in the *Wexford Independent*. This newspaper, with only eight printed pages, brought the people of Castlebridge world news, Irish reports and a sampling of local news. The local news usually consisted of reports from the courts or the meetings of the board of guardians. Sadly we are speaking of a period less than a decade after the Famine and Black 47 so the workhouse still dominated many lives. Yet it is amazing how resilient the people must have been. Castlebridge was close to completing its new church and, for those in the part of the parish at Ferrybank, the rising steeples of the twin churches would have been visible.

The year 1855 had its dramatic moments. There was a Tenants Rights Meeting held in Wexford in January. The ship *Hollyhock* out of Boston was shipwrecked off Carne. On 8 February there was such a heavy snow that the post from Dublin was delayed by several days, as roads were impassable and they ended up sending the mail by horse rider. The widow Clancy found a packet of about seventy letters at Kyle, probably dropped by an Irish-style pony express rider. Among the letters and newspapers were some containing a substantial amount of money. There is no record of the good lady being rewarded.

At the Spring Assizes the grand jury – a precursor of a county council – agreed to send an address to Sir Robert McClure, who had been born in Wexford, on his discovery of the North West Passage.

The breakwater in Wexford Harbour was being constructed and, in the summer of 1855, had about 60 yards to be added for completion. Shipping would still have been one of the more popular modes of transport, although the railway was making inroads and the train from Harcourt Street in Dublin would get you to Wexford – around Carcur – leaving Dublin at 8 a.m. and arriving at 11.40 a.m. Not bad for a century and a half ago.

In the same year an active Home Rule Club went on their annual outing to Parnell's home at Avondale.

We often think of our ancestors as parochial people but looking back at the goods on offer in 1855 we should perhaps reconsider.

Among the shops and goods on offer in 1855 were floorboards from Norway at the premises of Michael Ennis on Custom House Quay. Unlike Ikea, these Scandinavian timber products would have come direct by ship to the harbour. In John Hayes' grocery shop at 81 North Main Street they were buying Shetland ling and Labrador herring. These offers remind us of gourmet palates and ocean-going trade. William Fortune of The Bullring was advertising a 'Cheap Sale' with novels, toys, carpets, briar pipes and souvenir views of Wexford on offer. He also had 'Britannia Metal Teapots' for 10s (that's about 60 cents).

Maybe this cosmopolitan atmosphere was not so unusual. We must remember that, at the time, Wexford was a major port with ships sailing to all points of the globe and no doubt many Castlebridge sons, not willing or able to farm the land, crewed these barques and brigs. In the decades prior to 1855 the seafaring tradition of Wexford Town had brought tragedy and death to Castlebridge parish. In the 1830s cholera spread worldwide. There is a story that a young sailor from Maudlintown in Wexford jumped from his ship off Curracloe. He carried the disease along the road from there back into Wexford and the deadly disease, which could kill in a day, cut down many people in the district.

On the social and family level in 1855 it was common for the ladies of all houses to knit stockings for the whole family and to make underclothes, shirts, bed linen and quilts. In the pre-television, age hands, young or old, were seldom idle.

People were entertained by travelling shows that performed in tents or in the rising number of parish halls.

WEXFORD AND VIRGINIA

We have no exact number of Wexford people sent to Virginia in the 1600s but there is reason to believe that the number was considerable. The journals of the American Irish Historical Society contain valuable lists of early colonists bearing Irish surnames. Wexford surnames are exceptionally well represented, indicating that emigration to Virginia from Wexford was by no means insignificant. Some of the names found in Virginia at the time include Edmund

Bolger, Garrett Brien, Richard Murphy, John Doyle, Henry Roche, Daniel Cavanegh, Edmund Murphy, Darby Byrne and Garrett Byrne. William Hutchin is recorded to have married a lady named Nancy Cavanaugh and John Murphy was a witness to the will of Charles Cavenah of Edgecome County probated in 1757.

The records of the bordering state of North Carolina have many Wexford surnames, particularly Murphy. In the first census, dated 1790, no less than seventy-two heads of families had the name Murphy. The Murphys were in North Carolina from an early date, and traces of people of this name could be found in place names from the city of Murfeesboro in Hertford County, in the eastern part of the State, to the town of Murphy, Cherokee County, in the extreme north-western part, on the border of Tennessee.

BROWNSWOOD

Mention Brownswood today and most Wexford people of a certain age will respond 'the san'. They are referring to the sanatorium that was located there in the mid-1900s. It later became a medical hospital and then a nursing home. Originally there was a castle of the Browne family near the site. Patrick Browne lived there in the seventeenth century. The castle was attacked by George Cooke, Cromwellian Governor of Wexford, and all the inhabitants slain in 1650. The Brownswood Estate was purchased by Colonel Rochford in the 1800s and later sold to Captain Jeremiah Lonsdale Pounden who was married to Jane Stewart the daughter of the Earl of Moray – as referred to in a Scottish tune. Their daughter Evelyn, who became Baroness Gray, carried out great improvements to the house; laying out gardens and building magnificent stables. She was a great party person and, on one occasion, hung Chinese lanterns along the avenue for an 'At Home', as the party was called. Guests included Fanny Moody, a famous opera singer, and her husband Charles Mansergh. Brownswood had the distinction of being the first residence in the county to be fitted with electric lighting. The house was sold to the Wexford Board of Health in 1927.

3

PEOPLE

Like most counties, Wexford has a wide range of personalities who contributed over the centuries to make us what we are. Rather than recall the well-known names of history, local or national, we will provide pen portraits of a sprinkling of lesser-known, but equally important, people who gained some notoriety in County Wexford, alongside some who, though born in this south-east corner of Ireland, spread their wings to flourish elsewhere.

DAVID BEATTY

In the Napoleonic wars, David Beatty served under Wellington in the Peninsular War and raised, at his own expense, a troop known as the Healthfield Horse, named after the family estate in County Wexford. But his is not the story that captured the imagination of Wexford.

On the Beatty family vault, situated in Killurin churchyard, there was an inscription, which read: 'Here also, on October 9th 1846 was interred Elizabeth, Mrs David Beatty (nee Martin) of Borodale.' Lady Beatty, who was aged 29 years, was reputedly interred wearing her personal jewellery.

The story continues that the family butler, aware of this, decided to recover these valuable items and made his way that night to the vault. By candle or lamplight, he removed the coffin lid and, because he had some difficulty removing a ring, is said to have attempted to amputate her finger. The shock restored Lady Beatty to her senses, having been in some sort of a coma. Needless to say the butler took to his heels, either in terror or to escape the consequences, and was not seen again.

The lady took stock of her situation and appears to have walked the mile and a half to her home at Heathfield. One can but wonder at the consternation of staff and family at this unearthly re-appearance of a woman thought dead and buried.

However things went, she resumed a normal life only to die about eighteen months later. Her second death was recorded as being on 2 March 1848 at the age of 32 years.

The discrepancy in ages is usually explained by the lack of birth certificates and so the recorder would have just asked a family member what her age was and written that information into the register.

JAMES CARDIFF

James Cardiff, a young Protestant, lived in County Wexford in the 1790s. He was a well-educated young man. In fact, he was only recently returned from college when his parents died and left him a considerable tract of land. In 1797, Cardiff was seen as a generally good person but given to pranks and high spirits. It was just such high spirits that bring him to our attention two centuries later.

The 1790s were turbulent times in the county. There were a number of units of yeomen in the area and these often held marches and training days. One such unit, under Colonel Forde, was on parade in the area of Coolgreany and heading home via Scarnagh. James Cardiff was out shooting game and thought it a bit of fun to discharge his gun over the heads of the yeomen.

Colonel Forde was not amused and, following the testimony of a local named Doran, he arrested Cardiff and brought him to Wexford. Ironically, Colonel Forde was Cardiff's uncle but, on his evidence and that of Mr Doran, the accused was found guilty and sentenced to death.

Hundreds of people from North Wexford attended the execution and were shocked that the young man was to die on the word of his uncle.

The funeral procession, returning north, must have been a spectacular sight, with hundreds of mourners on horseback. At Ballyfad House they found the gates locked. They broke them open and placed the young man's coffin on the steps of the house and called

Colonel Forde out to witness the results of his handiwork. Forde did not come forth but it was said that Cardiff's blood flowed and stained the steps of the house. The body was then taken and buried at Kilninor cemetery.

Legend states that the stain remained on the steps of Ballyfad and, in 1828 when the owner had the step turned over, the stain re-appeared on the exposed surface.

MARTIN CASH

Cash was born in Enniscorthy and brought up in a wealthy family. He is said to have fallen in love with a young woman who earned a living by making straw hats and bonnets. However, a man named Jessop made advances to his sweetheart and, in a jealous rage, Cash shot him. Cash was sentenced to seven years' penal transportation. He left Cork Harbour on board the *Marquis of Huntley* with 170 other convicts and arrived in Sydney on 10 February 1828. He was 'assigned' to Mr G. Bowman of Richmond and was transferred to Hunter River where he would be a stock rider for nine years. During this time he is believed to have inadvertently become involved in branding stolen cattle. Knowing the penalty if he was caught, he decided to depart for Van Diemen's Land. He was soon in trouble again and came before John Price the magistrate at Hobart Town. He was sentenced to two years, in addition to his original seven-year sentence, with four years' imprisonment with hard labour at Port Arthur. Cash briefly escaped and eighteen months were added to his time. Again he escaped, and almost made it across the Bass Strait, but was caught and faced ten years at Port Arthur a so-called 'escape proof colony'.

On Boxing Day 1842, Martin Cash, George Jones and Lawrence Kavenagh absconded from a work party and hid in dense scrub land. Swimming with their clothes tied in bundles above their heads, they made the other side but lost their bundles. The naked trio robbed a road gang's hut for clothing and began a twenty-month spree of bushranging, robbing mail coaches, homesteads and inns. They became known as Cash and Co.

Their reputation grew but, in August 1843, Cash discovered his partner Bessie was with another man in Hobart. He swore to kill them both and he made his way to Hobart. On 29 August 1843 he was spotted in Hobart near the old Commodore Inn and a gunfight ensued. Constable Peter Winstanley was shot by Cash and died two days later. Cash was tried for murder in September 1843 and found guilty. He was sentenced to death by hanging, but a last-minute reprieve saw him sentenced to transportation for life to Norfolk Island. There he eventually became a trustee, and later a constable. He married in 1854, and was granted his ticket of leave later that year.

Between 1854 and 1856 he was an overseer in the Royal Hobart Botanical Gardens and it was during this time that he had a daughter named Monique. Subsequently he travelled to Christchurch, New Zealand, where he kept several brothels in 1860, and became a free man in 1863. Cash died in his bed in Glenorcht, Tasmania, in 1877. He is one of the only bushrangers to die of old age.

THE DEVEREUXES OF UTICA, NEW YORK

The final years of the eighteenth century were times of great movement among the citizens of the world. The United States of America were seen as the Promised Land. Revolutionary France was another attraction, particularly for people living in a land where they were persecuted for their religion. In such a climate many people left Ireland.

In 1795 John Devereux of Wexford decided to leave his native land and seek his fortune in France. There, he learned to play the fiddle and to dance. With these qualifications he headed for the New World, landing in New York in 1797.

Over the next few years John Devereux travelled around the small towns of New York, earning his living as a dancing master. In this time he recalled that he 'danced a thousand dollars out of the Yankees'.

With those 1,000 dollars he opened a general store and finally settled down in Utica in 1802. The business proved very popular and Devereux's store became the gathering place for newly arrived Irish exiles.

Many of these migrants were Catholics and, with no church in the town, the Devereux home became the Mass house and the base for visiting missioners. John and his brother Nicholas, who had joined him from Wexford, were also busy on the religious front, reading prayers and teaching catechism.

Indeed Nicholas is said to have spent the first fifteen minutes of each day reading the Bible. He offered prizes to any boy who could recite St John's Gospel and a new suit of clothes was on offer to any boy who could repeat the text of all four Gospels.

Later, he had printing plates brought over from Dublin and produced copies of the Douai New Testament, which he distributed free to all who would accept them. Over the years these plates formed the basis for the largest Catholic publications business in the United States, producing 20,000 copies in 1840.

One of the distinguished visitors to the Devereux house in Utica at that time was Father Theobald Matthew, the famous temperance priest. Indeed, it is recorded by Nicholas Devereux's wife that, 'more than 1,000 people took the pledge in my parlour and halls' on that day.

Religion did not interfere with business for the Devereux brothers and they amassed quite a fortune over the years.

Nicholas set up eight Franciscans on a 500-acre farm at Ellincottville and later spent $5,000 establishing St Bonaventure College at Allegany, New York. Nicholas was invited to Rome and received by Pope Pius IX and his cardinals at the time of the proclamation of the Dogma of the Immaculate Conception.

He was also the first subscriber to a college for US students in Rome and he gave $10,000 to establish the first Catholic church in Connecticut, at Hartford.

EILEEN GRAY

Kathleen Eileen Moray Gray was an Irish-born furniture designer and architect and a pioneer of the Modern Movement in architecture.

Eileen Gray was born Katherine Eileen Moray Smith on 9 August 1878, near Enniscorthy. Her father, James McLaren Smith, was a painter who encouraged his daughter's artistic interests. Her mother, Eveleen Pounden, separated from her husband in 1888. Eveleen was a granddaughter of the Tenth Earl of Moray and she became Baroness Gray in 1895, after which she changed her children's surname to Gray. Eileen spent her childhood in Ireland or South Kensington in London.

In 1898, Gray attended classes at the Slade School of Fine Art, where she studied painting. In 1900 her father died and she went to Paris with her mother where she attended the Exposition Universelle, celebrating the achievements of the past century. Gray continued her studies at the Académie Julian and the Académie Colarossi in Paris. In 1924 Gray, in collaboration with Jean Badovici, began work on a house they called E-1027 in southern France. The odd name comes from the names of the couple – E for Eileen, 10 for Jean (J as tenth letter of the alphabet), 2 for Badovici and 7 for Gray. Gray designed the furniture as well as collaborating with Badovici on its structure. The French Government have subsequently designated this house a French National Cultural Monument. Gray is also celebrated for her innovative furniture design.

FRANCIS MURPHY

Francis Murphy was born in Tagoat, County Wexford, on 24 April 1836. His father, a tenant farmer, died before the boy was born, leaving him to be raised by his mother. He began his education at a local school but was an unwilling scholar and left soon after to enter service with his mother's landlord. This service continued until Francis was 16 years old and decided to seek his fortune in America.

Arriving at New York, the young Murphy promptly squandered what little capital he had brought with him and began drifting from job to job. He eventually settled as a labourer on a farm in upstate New York, where his luck changed. After a short courtship he married the daughter of his employer and raised a number of children.

On the early death of his wife, Francis re-married. This time to a Mrs Fisher who was a prominent figure in the Ladies Temperance Movement.

With the outbreak of the Civil War, he enlisted as a private in the 92nd New York Infantry and served for three years.

After the war, with financial assistance from his brother who had also gone to America, Francis became the owner of a hotel in Portland. Despite his earlier work for temperance, or perhaps because of it, Murphy acquired a strong taste for alcohol. This became his downfall, leading to business failure, debts and imprisonment.

While detained in the local jail, he was visited by Captain Cyrus Sturdevant who convinced him to take the pledge and forsake the demon drink. Upon release from prison, Francis was an enthusiastic attender at temperance meetings where he testified to the evils of drink.

So popular and successful was this reformed drinker that he became president of the State Reform Club. He adopted a blue ribbon as a temperance badge and framed a pledge of his own, The Murphy Pledge.

In one ten-week period in 1876, Francis Murphy is reputed to have caused 40,000 men to take the pledge, raised $15,000 dollars for the movement and caused 500 saloons to close through lack of drinkers.

His fame spread beyond America. On a tour of Ireland, Scotland and England, he was received by Queen Victoria. He preached temperance in Canada and Australia and served as special chaplain to the 5th Pennsylvania Volunteers during the Spanish-American War.

During his long career in the temperance movement, Francis Murphy of Tagoat is credited with having addressed over 25,000 public meetings and caused more than 12 million men to swear off alcoholic drink.

Although he was a firm believer in temperance, Murphy did not support either the Prohibition Party or the Anti-Saloon League in their efforts to use legislation to curb drinking. Francis Murphy believed that it was only by conscious personal effort that people could give up alcohol.

QUAKERS IN WEXFORD

Quakerism was introduced to Ireland by William Edmondson and its message of peace soon spread throughout the country. In the post-Cromwellian era this found sound footing in County Wexford.

Among the Quaker settlers were: the Poole family; Thomas Holme, who would become surveyor general to William Penn in Pennsylvania; the Randalls, who would settle in The Deeps; the Haughtons; the Tottenhams; and the Williams, among others.

The first Friends' Meeting to be held in Wexford took place at The Deeps in the home of Francis Randall who later built a Meeting House at nearby Edermine. He was a man much loved by all with whom he had contact.

Initially the society members met mainly in private houses but, as numbers increased, Meeting Houses were built at Edermine, Forrest (near Taghmon), Cooladine, Ross, Wexford Town and Enniscorthy. The Enniscorthy house was the last one remaining but, throughout the county, several well-kept burial grounds remain in use.

The Quakers were of a strong and resolute breed who endured much hardship and persecution. Francis Randall suffered more than once. For meeting at James Beckett's house at Ross he was beaten and thrust out of the town having been beaten by a musket. He suffered imprisonment for two years in Wexford gaol along with Israel Davis and Richard Poole because he would not pay fees to the Established Church. Poole died in the gaol.

The Quakers were also well known for their ability in farming and their integrity in business. In the eighteenth century Arthur Young, travelling through Ireland, related: 'A farmer I talked to said of them "the Quakers be very cunning and divil a bit of bad land will they hire".'

The rebellion of 1798 saw their peaceable nature tested. Dinah Goff, of Horetown, went through terrifying experiences with the undaunted faith and courage of any Quaker family. At Horetown House, many local people were in their employment. Some left them to take service with the insurgent army and many difficulties arose. Dinah's relates:

> About ten days before the Rebellion broke out a gentleman residing near told my father that in a few days the country would be in a state of insurrection and advised my father to remove, with his family, by way of a boat which this gentleman had lying at Duncannon fort ready to set sail for Wales. My father decided, after deep thought, it was wise to remain at home placing confidence in Him who alone can protect.

The Goff's owned the mansion and estate of Horetown and were constantly required to provide provisions for the insurgents. In her diary Dinah notes, 'Two servants were forced to join the rebels to save their lives but, on my mother seeing their pikes she said she would not allow such things into the house, so every night they left them outside the door.' In spite of such trials the family remained in their house, often surrounded by an armed force.

On Sundays the younger members walked to Forrest, 3 miles away, for the Friends Meeting. Hundreds were fed on the lawn of Horetown House.

The scholarship and interest in local history fostered by the Friends inspired Jacob Poole, who left us a full glossary of the Forth-Bargy dialect of Yola. The manuscript is preserved in the Friends' Meeting House in Dublin.

PATRICK AND NATHANIEL TRACEY

Patrick Tracey was a sailor born in Wexford in 1711, 'a little village on the east coast of the Emerald Isle'. In 1735 he left his native land and sailed, like many others, to America. His port of destination was Newburyport in Massachusetts.

He came from Ireland penniless and went to work as a sailor on ships built in Newburyport Harbor. He became a ship's officer, a navigator, a master and finally an owner.

He married Hannah Gookin, a minister's daughter and in 1751 his son, Nathaniel Tracey, was born. In due time Nathaniel was sent to Harvard College, matriculating with the class of 1769. Nathaniel Tracey would be a prominent name in the Revolutionary War. He would donate a large sum of money to the continental coffers and, along with a brother-in-law, he operated thirty-five sailing vessels, many of them operating as privateers.

During this time, Nathaniel would entertain, among others, George Washington and Lafayette at his large home in Newburyport. The house would later become a public library.

His sister, also called Hannah, was noted as a beauty who had even turned the head of John Quincy Adams. She would marry

Jonathan Jackson, a delegate to the Continental Congress from Massachusetts and together they had nine children.

Of their children, Charles became a Justice of the Supreme Court of Massachusetts and James became a physician and later a founder of Massachusetts General Hospital. Patrick would be a founder of Merrimack Manufacturing Company, which would be instrumental in the foundation of the city of Lowell, and Frances married Francis Cabot Lowell who was a partner in the manufacturing enterprises.

Many of the most prominent Boston families of later generations, such as Cabot, Lowell, Lee, Putnam and Holmes, trace part of their ancestry back to the sailor from Wexford called Patrick Tracey. His portrait hangs in the National Gallery of Art in Washington.

WAS ZORRO FROM WEXFORD?

We know that the familiar face of Zorro with the black clothes, rapier and mask is a fictional character but what we seldom realise is that, like many heroes of fiction, he may have a real-life inspiration. Not only is this true but the inspiration in question might just stem from County Wexford.

According to the book *The Irish Zorro* by Gerard Ronan, the story begins with Richard Lamport who had helped pilot Spanish forces into Kinsale in support of Hugh O'Neill's rebellion in the early 1600s. William was from Wexford and may have honed those seafaring skills while sailing around the then busy port. A devout Catholic, he had witnessed the persecution of his fellow religionists and neighbours under Elizabeth I, where their beliefs equated to treason. His cousin Peter Lombard had promised a 'crusade indulgence' to those taking part in the rebellion against the queen when he was Primate of Ireland. This appears similar to the Pope urging the knights on to crusades six centuries earlier.

Unfortunately, the rebellion failed and Richard ended up transporting defeated Irish rebels to the Continent where many joined the Spanish forces. After this he returned to Wexford and was fortunate that his arrival corresponded with a boom in herring fishing. He was soon 'back in business' as a merchant. He married

Allison, the daughter of Lord Sutton, so we must assume that he had become quite wealthy from the herring trade or maybe from something less reputable. Ronan tells us that Sutton, with his ship *Le Handymade de Villa Wexford*, was actively involved in smuggling and that Richard may have become acquainted with his future father-in-law through this trade.

Whatever the circumstance, Allison moved, along with her much older husband, from her country residence to Wexford Town. Ronan gives a less-than-glamorous picture of the seventeenth-century Wexford as 'noisy and unhealthy ... faction fights were not uncommon outside the local brothels and alehouses'. He refers to the stink from tanning pits and curing houses, raw sewage in feculent and verminous lanes that ran steeply downhill and about 1,000 souls living in 'the quarter moon of the town walls'. The couple had three sons and a daughter of whom William was the second, born on 25 February 1615. Unfortunately for the family and most others in Wexford this period saw much anti-Catholic legislation introduced with those of the religion purged from the legal profession and others.

In William's youth the sport of bull baiting, which would give its name to The Bulling in modern Wexford, was introduced. There was much more interest in Spain at this time with the hope of Felipe IV influencing a restoration of Catholic power in Europe. In fact we have references in other works to the Spanish flag being hoisted on Wexford Castle. Richard sailed for Spain on what appears to have been a long trip and his son would later allude to 'services performed on behalf of Your Majesty' to the Spanish king. Allison died during this absence and the children went into the care of relatives. Richard returned to Wexford some time later and only then learned of his wife's death. Rather than taking on the care of the children, he decided to join the priesthood and moved into the house of Father William Devereux, a well-known schoolmaster in Wexford. With the relaxation of anti-Catholic laws Devereux became parish priest of Wexford. He also set about drafting a catechism for the local children.

William Lamport, meanwhile, was tutored by an Augustinian named Thomas Furlong in reading, writing and Latin. In 1625 his education continued under two Franciscans – Anthony Turner and Walter Cheevers – at their church in High Street. At the age of just 11 years, William entered a Jesuit college in Back Lane in Dublin, indicating the obvious family influence of the Lamports. From there he went to London where he was arrested for treason. Escaping under mysterious circumstances, William ended up on a ship that was taken by pirates and, rather than be returned to England, he joined with his captors. His Wexford upbringing and, no doubt, his involvement in his father's shipping enterprises evidently contributed to his abilities in this sphere.

From his pirate days he went to the Continent and enjoyed many adventures, including combat in the Siege of La Rochelle and the Battle of Nördlingen. Next we hear of him in Mexico, where he fell foul of The Inquisition because of his plans regarding abolishing slavery and seeking Mexican independence. To the dreaded Inquisition he pointed out his Catholic upbringing in Wexford, his baptism in the parish of St Peter in that town and his confirmation by Bishop Rothe.

Once again there is a miraculous escape on Christmas night in 1650. His adventures became the stuff of legend and inspired novels and plays. Many consider that Zorro, as created by Johnston McCully in 1919, owes much to the life and adventures of Wexford's William Lamport, although there are many other contenders for that honour.

In 2013 Wexford consolidated this connection by inaugurating a Zorrofest in the town.

Note: Like many family names, Lamport had different spellings over time and is now more commonly known as Lambert.

It is interesting to note that while William was enjoying his adventures in Mexico, Wexford was being ravaged by Oliver Cromwell and, incidentally, the reference to a population of 1,000 in the early 1600s makes the later claim of 2,000 killed only forty years later at the Market Cross by Cromwell's men less than likely.

OTHER PEOPLE

Listed below are a number of interesting people for whom we have not been able to obtain full details but are worthy of recognition.

Barry, John, parish priest of Crossabeg, died, 1868. He was curate in the parish of Wexford at the time of the first outbreak of the first cholera in 1832, where he laboured incessantly, administering relief and religious consolation to his afflicted people.

Cronin, Anthony was born in Enniscorthy in 1928. He is a poet, novelist and arts activist. He has also written biographies of Brian O'Nolan and Samuel Beckett. He persuaded Charles Haughey to found Aosdána, the Arts Council, and support struggling writers, composers and artists with the annuity known as the Cnuas. He was involved in organising the first ever Bloomsday and has produced television programmes including *Between Two Canals* and *Flann O'Brien – Man of Parts*.

Danby, Francis ARA, was the son of a small tenant farmer, and was born at Loughard, near Killinick in 1793. His family removing to Dublin, he received the principles of his art education there, and went to London. An artist of a poetical and creative genius, he was a constant exhibitor at the Royal Academy, from 1821 to 1830. Mr Danby died at the 'Shell House', Exmouth, Devonshire in 1861, aged 61 years.

De Clonard (The Countess) died at Vendome, France in January 1857. Her ladyship's maiden name was Crosbie and she was born at Ballinagee near Wexford.

Devereux, John Thomas, was part of a family that helped to establish Wexford's prosperity in the nineteenth century. The family's ships sailed to many foreign ports and helped in the export of Irish goods. John Thomas was often referred to as a man of 'shrewd insight, sound capacity and upright principle'. He was as much a familiar figure in Dublin and London as he was in his native Wexford. His success was based on foresight and sound calculation in the London Corn Exchange. He moved into politics in 1847 with the Repeal Movement waning and was returned unopposed for the Wexford Borough in that year and again in July 1852 and March 1857. He was a Liberal and a member of the parliamentary party known as 'The Brass Band'. Charles

Gavin Duffy noted his 'character of independence' in voting with him, Lucas and McMahon among other Irish politicians, as an 'independent opposition'. He died in 1886 at the age of 85 years. The then 'high altar' in the Church of the Immaculate Conception was set up as a memorial to his munificence.

Donovan, Captain, who survived an attack by the Kellymount Gang. The Kellymount Gang was a band of desperados, commanded by a leader named Brennan, who kept the south of the country in a state of terror. Their raids extended over several counties in Leinster and Munster. In January 1740, a number of gentlemen and their retainers formed themselves into a company and attacked the gang in their stronghold. A battle ensued and Brennan was killed. His followers dispersed. The towns and neighbourhoods of County Wexford had not escaped the depredations of the gang, however, and have it on record that they visited the neighbourhood of Enniscorthy and attacked the residence of Captain Donovan, at Clonmore, Bree. Donovan had served with honour in many campaigns and, it is stated that, to keep his warlike spirit up, he used to head parties in pursuit of the 'Gang.' The attack made on Donovan's residence came at night, with loud shouts and threatened to murder all in the house. The old soldier and his servants barricaded the house and made a gallant defence, finally succeeding in driving the marauders away. In defending his house Captain Donovan was wounded by a gunshot in the eye, the sight of which he lost.

Graves, William of New Ross was the first Irishman to become mayor of Liverpool. He had been born in 1818 and was educated at a private school in the town. He married Elizabeth Haughton and later settled in Liverpool where he became a prosperous merchant. His primary business was as a shipowner. He became Liverpool's first citizen in the year 1861 and, four years later, he became a Conservative MP for the borough. His business interests included the London & North Western Railway and the Pacific Navigation Company. He was also commodore of the Mersey Yacht Club. He entertained members of the royal family on visits to the city and Queen Victoria sent a letter of sympathy on his death. A monument was erected to his honour in Liverpool.

Handley, Edward, gamekeeper on the Wilton estates, was murdered as he was returning home from the town of Enniscorthy in 1839. Two brothers of the name of Kelly were tried for the murder and acquitted. They afterwards emigrated.

Harvey, Captain James JP, died in 1873. Captain Harvey served in the Guards at Waterloo, and took part in the final and crowning charge, when the command of 'Up, Guards, and at them' was given. He succeeded Colonel Pigott as Master of the Wexford Hunt, an office he held for a few seasons, and it is a coincidence that their deaths took place on the same date in the same month.

Jackman, James, was tried at Wexford Spring Assizes in 1833. Jackman was found guilty of aiding and assisting in the murder of John Roche, of Old Court, Wexford. Jackman's father had formerly been in possession of the farm held by Roche, but was dispossessed for non-payment of rent. Jackman was sentenced to be hung on 4 March but was 'respited' until 25th. Previous to that date, however, his sentence was commuted to transportation for life and he was removed from Wexford Gaol on 28 March.

'Marino nan'. Today we approach a total ban on smoking in public places. Back in 1937 such was not the case. Smoking was encouraged in all sorts of ways and Marino Cigarettes used one interesting advertising ploy – they had a mysterious stranger travel the land and accost people on the streets. Marino man, as he was known, walked about and asked people to produce a packet of Marino cigarettes. Those who had them got a voucher for a free ticket in the Irish Hospital sweepstakes – the lotto of yesteryear. Among the lucky ones in 1937 were – J. Barker of 36 South Main Street, J. Lewis of 6 Antelope Road, T. Kelly of 10 Monck Street, Garda McKee of George's Street Barracks, T. Byrne of The Avenue Gorey, Garda Prior of New Ross and T. Tobin of Enniscorthy. I wonder if any of them won the sweep.

O'Leary, Thomas, died at Galena, Illinois, America, in 1877. He was a native of Wexford and emigrated with his parents in 1828, when he was only 10 years of age. From his early manhood he was identified with the prosperity of his adopted city. In 1860 he was elected an alderman, which office he held up to 1863, when he was appointed police marshal, a position he held until his death. The newspapers of Galena stated that his funeral was the largest ever seen in their city, being attended by the mayor and council, the fire brigade, and all the societies belonging to the city.

O'Neill, Daniel, proprietor of the Pittsburgh (United States) *Despatch* newspaper, died in 1877. Mr O'Neill was a native of the County Wexford, being born at Cloughbawn, Barony of Bantry, on New Year's Day, 1830. His father, Mr Hugh O'Neill, was principal of a school there, which had been established by the grandfather of the present Lord Carew, and from which emanated some good scholars and successful writers.

Oustainge, Oscar Henry, Professor of Dancing, died suddenly at New Ross in 1860. He had been in Enniscorthy the previous day, making arrangements to open an academy in that town. He was a native of Wexford (though of French extraction), where his father kept an academy in the early part of the twentieth century.

Percival, Edward, a native of County Wexford, was killed in action, 1813. The plaque in his honour at St Iberius' church in Wexford reads:

> Sacred to the memory of Mr Edward Percival late Master's Mate in the Royal Navy, who fell gallantly in his country's cause in an attack upon an enemy of far superior force, in a boat belonging to His Majesty's Frigate 'Havannah' on 6 January 1813, on the coast of Istria, in the Adriatic aged 21 years. His amiable heart and noble disposition secured him the esteem and friendship of all who knew him, whilst his public conduct ever endeared him to the approbation of those officers with whom he served, in testimony whereof, the Captain and Officers of the 'Havanah', have caused this monument to be erected to his memory, as a sincere tribute to departed worth, as well as of their admiration of the heroic manner in which he fell.

Rea, Stephen, printer, died at Wellington Road, Liverpool, in 1858. He was a native of Wexford (where he served his time), the second son of Mr Stephen Rea, of the Customs, and grandson of Captain William Hore, of the 92nd Regiment of Highlanders.

Roche, William Sylvester, surgeon, lost his life in a railway accident at London Bridge railway station in 1874. Surgeon Roche was a native of the parish of Adamstown, County Wexford, and was a comparatively young man when he met with the accident that deprived him of life. During the war with Russia he distinguished himself in the naval service of his country, both in the Baltic and Black seas, and for which he received medals. He was also decorated with the Turkish Order of Medjide.

Sinnott, John, died in the Gorey Workhouse, aged 16 years in 1857. He was only 26 inches tall.

Skelton, Dr James of Enniscorthy, died at the age of 100 years in 1844.

4

EVENTS

NINETEENTH-CENTURY CIRCUSES

From late spring until early autumn, the people of County Wexford were entertained by the travelling circus. This class of show can be greatly underestimated by the modern mind because of our ease of travel. We must remember that in those far-off days most people travelled only as far as they could comfortably walk. Few had horses or even donkeys and those who did would only use such precious beasts for essential travel, usually for business reasons. The coming of the bicycle would increase the range of travel and many social historians credit this invention with the widening of the family gene pool, with suitors moving outside their townland or village for a partner.

In the 1870s Powell & Clarke's Circus was eagerly anticipated in County Wexford each year. The main attraction was Johnny Patterson, billed as 'The Irish Clown', whose name was a household word in rural Ireland. Eventually the island proved too small for him and he moved to America where he toured with Barnum & Bailey's.

A little over a decade later, County Wexford was enthralled with Lloyd's Circus, which arrived in June 1885. By this time Patterson had returned to Ireland and was an attraction with Lloyd's. In addition they boasted Fanny Ouri as 'the female Sampson'. This show also featured the Lloyd Brothers who 'somersaulted on ropes while playing musical instruments'.

The next circus to grace our fields came in the following year. This was Ginnett's Circus and its prime feature was a spectacular procession of impressive horses. The show had previously toured America so we, in this small county, were getting class, international fare.

There appears to have been no end to the array of touring circuses in those latter decades of the nineteenth century. We hear of Batty's; Davie's, Poole & Boscoe; as well as Hanneford's and the wonderfully named Buff Bill's. One wonders if the latter was a Wild West show.

It was these circuses that originally brought the forerunner of cinema to the people of rural Ireland. The 'moving picture show' usually occurred after the live acts each night. Traditionally these were short comic acts but later, when so many Wexford men were fighting in South Africa, battle scenes from the Boer War featured.

In an interesting County Wexford footnote, it is recorded that when Lloyd's Circus finally disbanded, the proprietor, Jemmy Lloyd, moved into the haulage business. He secured the haulage contract connected with the New Ross water supply from Ballyleigh Reservoir.

AIRBORNE WEXFORD

The first aerial ascent in County Wexford took place by balloon in 1870. Described as an 'aeronaut', Mister Hodman made his ascent at Drinagh, just south of Wexford Town, on land where the Wexford Militia trained. The event, as might be expected, attracted very large crowds. On first going up the balloon began to drift out to sea but luckily a change in wind direction brought the vessel back in to Drinagh. As always, such feats of daring must have attracted the ladies. In fact, it transpired that a passenger in the balloon was arrested at Cobh some weeks later while trying to gain passage to America – it appears that on his visit to Wexford he had contracted a bigamous marriage to a local girl.

The first aeroplane to visit the county arrived in 1910 and was at the New Ross Agricultural Show. Not wishing to give free view of an object that could be charged, for the owners maintained a cloak of secrecy over the event. The aeroplane arrived in New Ross by rail and brought to the showgrounds under cover of darkness. The show committee paid £ 0 for the contract and advertised the vehicle as 'the wonder of the age'. At the show it was kept under canvas and patrons paid sixpence each to go in to see it. Many were attracted by the buzzing as the propeller was whirled. Special trains were laid on to bring crowds to New Ross for the spectacle and extra police were on duty to control the throng. In the afternoon cheered erupted as the aeroplane was wheeled out and further cheering greeted the airman as he took his seat. Then, with great excitement from the crowd, the machine ran along the grass gathering speed. People watched with bated breath. But to no avail. It did not take to the air. Two more attempts were made but these also failed and the very disappointed crowds left the field. Some saw it as proof that man could not fly. The next day the aeroplane was brought back to the railway but it is said that few even bothered to acknowledge it.

Two years later the first 'flying' aeroplane was witnessed in County Wexford. In May 1912 our initial meeting with air travel came about because a plane had to make a forced landing in a field at Monageer near Enniscorthy. Mister Corbett-Wilson from Kilkenny had flown across from England and this was something of a sensation. In the best stiff-upper-lip tradition, he followed this mishap by journeying into Enniscorthy, where he had some breakfast and contacted some French engineers to come and carry out repairs. Corbett-Wilson travelled home by car after having the aeroplane brought into the town attended by big crowds. The mechanics arrived two days later. They could not speak English and the locals had no French so they were in a quandary – no one understood why these men were in Enniscorthy. Eventually a dentist called Briscoe, who had spent some time in Paris, intervened and it was established that they were there to fix the aeroplane and work commenced. When repairs were completed Corbett-Wilson returned and, in gratitude to the people, he offered to give an exhibition flight in the Showgrounds in aid of the fund to repair the cathedral spire. This took place on Ascension Thursday – surely a good omen – 1912 and thus was the first successful aeroplane flight in County Wexford. Corbett-Wilson went on to fly as an airman in the First World War, loosing his life in a reconnaissance mission.

LION HUNT IN TAGHMON

In the summer of 1939 two young Martin brothers and their friends, John Quigley and Mikey Carton, set off for a quiet afternoon fishing for roach in the local quarry near Taghmon. They had little on their minds but enjoying their leisure and some time had passed when Billy Martin shouted, 'Look at the lion, lads'. Looking up they saw a full-grown lioness approaching across Miss Roche's garden. Boys being boys, they started shaking the fishing rods at this animal, which was far out of its natural habitat in rural Ireland. The lioness watched them for a while.

Better sense soon overtook the four lads and they scrambled up a nearby cliff. On looking back, they saw the animal with its 'head erect against the evening skyline'. The beast had escaped only a short time before from Heckenberg's Circus, which was pitched in 'the circus field'. The boys recalled that the lioness then crossed the Wexford–Taghmon road opposite Mister Parle's and was not seen again that evening.

Next morning, Marks Redmond arrived for work at the farm of his employer Mr Winters at Ballintartan. He was told that the family had been 'up all night' because the escaped lioness was on his land and had killed a calf. He had taken a shot at her and believed that he had wounded her. They brought the other animals to safety and at about that time, Mr Fawsett, the lion keeper from the circus, arrived at the farm with another circus hand. On hearing the reports, the keeper went back to Taghmon to secure his rifle before the four men set out to follow the trail. By this time Marks Redmond was in possession of his employer's gun.

At the rath they sensed the animal was there but could not see her so the keeper fired his gun and flushed her from hiding. She sprang from the rath into a cornfield and the two men with guns gave chase, firing as they went. The lioness doubled back 'roaring' and headed for the rath again. The men kept firing and the beast fell, but they were out of ammunition and she was still alive. They sent back to the house for cartridges but Redmond feared that she might recover and head for the rath. Without ammunition he approached her from behind and dealt her a few 'heavy blows with an iron bar', stunning the beast. On the arrival of fresh cartridges he went close and finished her with a single shot.

The circus moved on to Blackwater where the manager asserted that not only was it their Mr Fawsett who killed the lioness but that the circus staff had always been close on her trail. He said that the keeper suffered a nervous breakdown for having to destroy the animal that he had trained.

In the tradition of anything being entertaining, the dead lioness and the calf were exhibited at the circus in Blackwater with attention drawn to the wound on the calf inflicted by the predator's claw. The next day the lioness was skinned at Bellefield in Enniscorthy, with the pelt preserved by the circus. The lioness carcass was buried in a field outside the town, the calf already having been buried at Blackwater.

Despite fears aroused during the escape, the escapade boosted attendance at the circus in subsequent days, with huge crowds jamming the roads and one person saying he was attending after not 'being to a circus in thirty-five years'.

DANIEL O'CONNELL IN ENNISCORTHY

Daniel O'Connell, 'The Liberator', addressed a huge crowd at a field near Red Pat's Cross on the outskirts of Enniscorthy on 20 July 1843. Generations later referred to it as 'The Repeal Field'.

Thousands of people came from every part of Wexford and the adjoining counties to support the movement then sweeping the country for the Repeal of the Union with Great Britain.

O'Connell left Dublin and all along the road he received a hero's welcome. At Gorey, hundreds of horsemen, as well as pedestrians, came to meet him. At Camolin, he was met by Revd Edward Kavanagh of Ballyoughter and Camolin, with his parishioners, and also by Revd James Roche, parish priest of Ferns, and his two curates, Revd B.E. Meyler and Revd E. Brownrigg, and their parishioners. At Ferns, O'Connell was met by horsemen from Enniscorthy.

It was seven o'clock when he arrived at the residence of the Most Revd Dr Keating, Bishop of Ferns, where he was the honoured guest at a dinner party. Next morning huge crowds from all over the country gathered at Enniscorthy. At least 150 boatloads of people arrived by the Slaney from Wexford to attend the Repeal demonstration.

The newspaper *The Nation* stated:

> The people of Forth and Bargy, joined by the trades and inhabitants of Wexford, proceeded along the Edermine road with bands playing and colours flying, to where the procession was formed. Large masses from Taghmon, Gorey, Ferns, Oulart, Ballygarrett, Kilmuckridge, Kilcormack, Blackwater, Newtownbarry [Bunclody], Kilmyshall, Templeshambo [Ballindaggin], Ross, Tomacork, Clonegal, Carnew, and Kildavin, came into town headed by their bands playing appropriate airs.

Trade groups, such as smiths, slaters, masons and others, paraded to present a scroll to O'Connell.

Daniel O'Connell travelled via the Presentation Convent, Duffrey Gate, St Aidan's Cathedral, Main Street, Rafter Street and along the road from the Millpark to Saint John's Bridge to Tomduff.

Tens of thousands waited for hours in the Repeal Field before O'Connell's procession arrived and the celebrated guest was given a rousing reception.

A PAUPER FUNERAL

In 1914 there was a sad report in the local newspapers concerning the way in which paupers were treated in the county, even in death.

Mr Hand reported to the New Ross Guardians that a large number of very respectable people had drawn his attention to what they considered a 'pathetic and at the same time very improper sight' observed in the town that week.

He referred to a hearse going through the town with two coffins 'crammed in'. These contained the remains of two deceased paupers. To add to the 'horrible spectacle' the coffins were bound around with tar ropes.

A Mr Breen asked 'Were they dead?' to which Mr Hand responded that there should be more respect. The chairman noted that he was sure no disrespect was intended. Mr Lennon said that he had enquired about this burial policy and was advised that friends of both parties were satisfied before the coffins were placed in the hearse.

Mr Egan said that the board was responsible for giving a decent burial to such poor people. He recalled the rhyme:

Rattle his bones over the stones,
He is only a pauper whom nobody owns.

He noted that a pauper has a soul like anyone else and that such scandals should no longer occur. The board agreed.

THE 'BIG SNOW'

The snow and frost that commenced on the eve of Twelfth Day 1814 was thought to have been the most severe since the 'Big Frost' of 1740. The weather had been mild, with little rain. However, on New Year's Day 1814 the wind veered to the east, with an overcast sky. On the evening of 5 January the wind rose and snow fell heavily for eighteen hours, covering the country to a depth of 3 or 4ft – and where snow-drifts formed, the depth was from 10 to 20ft. Great difficulty was experienced in recovering sheep from the fields. On the 7th the frost became intense, and the snow fell heavily at intervals, but it was remarkably dry and crisp, and the sun shone out brightly. This weather continued for three weeks, without any thaw. All outdoor work was suspended and many cattle and sheep perished. The roads were indistinguishable and several cabins were covered over and had to be abandoned by the inmates. The Slaney was frozen over from Ferry Carrig upwards, and was crossed by men and horses without danger. The whole of the extensive Wexford Harbour only exposed a narrow crooked line of open water in the tideway, and was covered with millions of wild waterfowls, very many of them kinds rarely seen here. The same was the case with the lakes of the county. The lake on Our Lady's Island attracted even more wildfowls, due to the water being nearly fresh and having no tide or natural outlet into the sea. The lake, 3 miles in length, was all frozen over to the thickness of 14 inches, except a semi-circular space of about quarter of a mile, where the birds were so numerous as to prevent the water from freezing by their perpetual motion, although millions of them died. All the fish in the lake perished also and, when a passage was cut into the sea in the following March, the bones of the perished wild birds and fish were said to have been as plentiful as shells on a cockle bed. There was not the slightest thaw until 1 February. Ague prevailed in much of the county during the following season, but other diseases were comparatively rare.

ATTACK OF THE WHITEFEET

A meeting of the magistrates of the county was held at Enniscorthy in 1833 to take into consideration the disturbed state of a portion of the county and to adopt measures for the suppression of midnight outrages. The meeting resolved that the police force of the county was to be increased by 100 men and that, in addition to the military stations of Wexford, Duncannon and New Ross, the government would be requested to have soldiers stationed at Enniscorthy, Newtownbarry, Templeudigan and the White Mountain; and also, to have an armed vessel stationed near New Ross, in order to protect the county from the depredations of the Whitefeet.

During 1832 and 1833, the Barony of Bantry, and parts of Scarawalsh and Shelburne, were very much disturbed by the proceedings of the Whitefeet, and some murders were committed by them, more particularly that of the Haddock's at Tomfarney. The police force of the disturbed districts had been increased, and continual night patrols were kept up.

On the night of 26 January 1833, the police on patrol duty in the neighbourhood of Adamstown came on an armed party of the Whitefeet, whom they challenged to surrender, but the Whitefeet refused. One of them levelled his gun at the police, but it misfired, upon which some of the patrol fired and a man named Thomas Gregory, who resided in the neighbourhood, was killed. The shooting of this man, the execution of Redmond and Jackman for the Tomfarney murders, and the transportation of many others, together with the active exertions of the local magistracy, put a stop to the depredations of the Whitefeet in this county, but they continued for some time longer on the borders of County Kilkenny.

On the same night of the above occurrence, an armed party of Whitefeet attacked the houses of William Power, and John and Moses Nowlan, in the parish of Whitechurch, Barony of Shelburne. They were threatened with death if they did not give up their lands.

ORANGE ATTACKS AT ENNISCORTHY IN 1839

Father James Roche was ordained by Bishop Keating and appointed to the cathedral in 1827. In 1833 a number of Orangemen assembled in the town and, in accordance with annual custom, erected a Liberty Tree in Market Square which they adorned with flowers. Some people were forced, under threat of violence, to bend their knee to this tree. Others planned an attack. These assembled at the Duffrey to prepare but Father Roche was alerted and rushed to the Duffrey to try and quell the crowd. Unfortunately, some people passing insulted the priest. Passions were inflamed and the crowd rushed down the hill to Market Square where they fell upon the Liberty Tree. Fierce hand-to-hand fighting ensued and only the re-appearance of Father Roche managed to prevent serious bloodshed. That was the last appearance of the Liberty Tree in Enniscorthy. Father Roche later transferred to Wexford where the twin churches are a monument to his work.

PARNELL IN ENNISCORTHY

We often think of politics in the 1800s as being clearly divided between the good guys and the bad guys. Here in Ireland we think back to Charles Stewart Parnell as the top good guy – at least until the Kitty O'Shea scandal. We also think that he had the undivided support of all Irish people. A report of a riot in Enniscorthy in 1880 gives the lie to this view.

In a *Freeman's Journal* story it was reported that the so-called 'hill siders' from the town pelted Parnell with rotten eggs, tore his trousers and broke up his meeting. This was not an isolated incident. Other meetings were disrupted in Castlecomer and in Limerick.

5

THE GREAT WAR

The world was in turmoil. The war that was to be 'over by Christmas' 1914 rumbled on and County Wexford men were fighting in foreign fields. An uprising had failed. But life went on. We take the middle week of December in 1917 for our snapshot of life in Wexford.

Fitzpatrick's at 94 North Main Street were suggesting wonderful Christmas presents, including pipes, cigarette cases and 'military wallets'. If you had 'defective teeth' you were asked to consult James Taylor at the dental surgery in Enniscorthy. But all was not well. Most towns were experiencing shortages of flour, sugar and even butter and milk.

Wexford beat Clare by 9 points to 5 in the All Ireland Football Championship at Croke Park. The Wexford team comprised of John O'Kennedy (captain), T. McGrath, G. O'Kennedy, P.J. Mackey, T. Mernagh, A. Doyle, J. Quinn, T. Doyle, T. Murphy, F. Furlong, J. Crowley, R. Reynolds, J. Byrne, M. Howlett and W. Hodgins.

WAGES

At the Enniscorthy Asylum the wages for staff were reported in local newspapers. The matron, Miss Kelly, had her salary increased by £10 to £70 per annum with allowances of £37 10*s*. The storekeeper, Thomas Kelly, also sought an increase of £10 on his annual salary of £60 a year plus £40 allowances. After being endorsed as very trustworthy and having over £20,000 of goods pass through his hands he got the rise.

CRIME

At Taghmon Petty Sessions there were a number of fines. Moses Breen was fined 2s 6d for drunkenness. Two farmers were fined for neglecting to dip sheep and four others were fined under the Lighting Act. In addition it was reported that:

> Two young fellows entered the Mr Foley's grocery and provision shop Main Street for the purpose of purchasing an apple. While waiting one of them snatched a box of dates and ran out of the shop followed by the other. In his excitement he dropped the dates on the street. Another boy picked them up and ran away. He escaped but the original pair were caught.

A lady at Porters Establishment buying bread put her change in her purse and put the latter in her pocket and left the shop. On reaching The Bullring she found the purse to be missing. This appears to have been part of pickpocketing epidemic.

Some boys got aboard the *Jane Mcoll* at the quay and stole two wrench handles and 'abstracted some iron from a door'. They then moved on to the *Tempest* and stole some more iron, which they are said to have 'sold in Wexford'.

ACCIDENTS

Denis Ryan of Clohamon suffered injury to his left hand when breaking coal for a threshing machine. The coal exploded and shattered his finger.

Matt Doyle of Ballycarney was struck in the eye by a piece of bush 'flying from a billhook'.

A Miss Rice of Horeswood suffered injury by shotgun pellets when her brother accidentally discharged it in the kitchen.

Bridget Stafford from Killinick was thrown from her donkey cart when 'the animal started and precipitated the lady to the ground'.

MEDICAL

A long advertisement stated that a visit by Mr Alexander Binnie would definitely end on Saturday 22 December. Binnie was offering Magneto Electric Treatment 'for pain and suffering'. The advisement quotes testimonials for curing all sorts of ailments from 'low spirits and general debility' to 'acute sciatica' and 'spine curvature'. The testaments were from parish priests around the country and justices of the peace. Consultations were said to be free. He had private rooms at Miss Mulrooneys at 7 Selskar Street in Wexford.

WORK

In Wexford Port, J.J. Stafford complained that 'there was unfair discrimination against Wexford owned vessels'. He said that sailors on Wexford vessels 'do not work after 5 o'clock and could knock off at 1 o'clock on Saturdays'. Those on foreign boats worked away as every hour counted to them. (Perhaps this was a case peculiar to all ports where people with families living locally spent some time with them.)

There were a number of reports – relatively few in the week in question – of death and injury in the war. But as we can see in Wexford, life was progressing with all the usual concerns.

6

IRELAND'S OWN

In 1902 County Wexford was part of the British Empire. British law prevailed and British magazines predominated. It was against this background that the Walsh family, originally from New Ross, decided to start a magazine. But this was to be no ordinary publication. The idea was to produce a magazine that combined the best of world information with all that was good in Ireland. The Walshes already had an advantage – being proprietors of the well-established *People* newspaper in Wexford, they had the staff and machinery to get going.

Magazines such as *John O'London's Weekly* and *Titbits* were top sellers in a field that was growing by the week. The market was increasing for a number of reasons. As a result of regular attendance at national schools, the general public was steadily growing more literate. The use of gas and later electricity for domestic lighting made it possible to read well into the night. Increasing mechanisation was making printing cheaper. It was in this atmosphere that *Ireland's Own* was born. From the very beginning it subtitled itself 'A Journal of Fiction Literature and General Information', a description that would last for ninety years.

The general mix of *Ireland's Own* was not unique. Many magazines and journals of that period carried jokes, romantic stories, serials, poems, fashion, etiquette and snippets. *Ireland's Own* had these, but they also printed the best of Irish literature and an Irish language column.

Over the years the rivals grew, shrivelled and died, but *Ireland's Own* continued. From the narrow back street in Wexford it moved to Dublin for a few years, but it was to return to its roots in the south east, from where copies were sent around the world.

DATE THE JOKES

From its very first issue, *Ireland's Own* has carried jokes. The official title of the page is 'Postcard Stories', and it is read by people from 9 or less to 90 or more. Try this short selection and see if you can put a year to them.

It was midnight, and the visitor showed no sign of leaving. He insisted on doing some bird impressions. 'Can you imitate a homing pigeon?' his hostess asked.

An old lady said she never knew why there were so many Smiths in the county until she saw a big factory called 'The Smith Manufacturing Company'.

First cannibal: 'Am I late for dinner?'
Second cannibal: 'Yes, everybody's eaten.'

The first was from 1957, the second from 1902 and the third from 1991. But could you tell?

FAR AND WIDE

Despite its production being located in a pair of narrow Wexford streets, *Ireland's Own* is known throughout the world. Its distribution addresses include every continent on earth, but its rather unique request to its readers to 'Pass on your copy to a friend', often increases its geographical spread.

As early as 1911 correspondents to the Readers Page had addresses ranging from Portugal to Bombay to Ohio and Buenos Aires.

7

CRIME

BROADWAY MURDER

This tale refers to a village in County Wexford and not the 'great white way' in New York, and it takes place when Eamon de Valera was making his mark, winning the East Clare election for Sinn Féin in 1917.

At a special court in Wexford, Sergeant Patrick Flaherty, noted as serving at Rosslare Pier, gave evidence of finding a body in Richards' Field. The body was found 'where a small stream intersects a public right of way'. There was a jagged wound in the neck and a blood-stained net cap and sun bonnet were near the body. 'The leaves of the briars and furze growing there were blood spattered.' The deceased was identified as Anne Moloney.

A witness named Ellen Sinnott was deposed and stated that on the night in question she had seen the accused at Richards' Field. In reply to her greeting he is said to have replied, 'I've done a bad job; I've killed old Anne and I suppose I'll be hung'.

Robert Cousins, son-in-law of the deceased, recalled meeting the accused about an hour after Mrs Moloney had left his house. He hailed him and, seeing blood on his clothes, asked what the matter was. Thomas replied, 'I am mad'.

Cousins said that the accused had been 'queer in his manner since his wife died last March' but that he was on good terms with the deceased. It was later stated by the accused's son that 'his father never had any quarrel with the deceased but in the last six weeks he had heard him say she was a fairy'.

Thomas Sinnott junior also testified that, on the night in question, Mary Cousins had called around the village looking for her mother (the deceased). After this he set out for his aunt's house at Trane and, on arriving, found his father and Robert Cousins outside. He asked what the matter was, to which Cousins replied that 'there is too much the matter'. He asked his father what was wrong and was told not to come near him if he wanted his life. He approached his father who ran off. Tripping on the road, the son helped him up and brought him to Broadway Cross.

John Purcell came out of his shop and the accused was heard to tell him that he had murdered Anne while showing him the knife. Purcell asked for the weapon and the accused handed it over, saying 'there is no man I would rather give it to'. Somers and Purcell then escorted the accused home where they made cocoa and waited for the police.

When the sergeant approached Thomas Sinnott and charged him with the crime he is said to have replied, 'What will I say? I will say anything you like. I murdered her. I don't deny it. I'm sorry for it. It was all her own fault.'

On being searched, the police found a quarter pound of tea labelled 'Edmund Doyle, family grocer, provision merchant, Broadway'. There were bloodstains on the collar of his coat and on his sleeve as well as mud stains which were similar to the clay on the bank of the stream. His boots were wet and 'covered with marl'. The sergeant found a penknife in the house, of which the large blade was stained with blood and mud.

The accused went to trial at the Leinster Winter Assizes.

KILLINICK KILLING

'Sanctuary' was the ironic name of the Cousins family home at Killinick in County Wexford. In the house lived John Cousins, his aunt Jane O'Brien and her son John.

On 26 March 1932 John Cousins went to visit his girlfriend Annie Maguire who lived nearby. His cousin John was also headed out for the night and he cycled into Wexford to go to the cinema. Cousins returned to the house around midnight. He had walked some of the journey with a friend called James Reilly. They parted company at the gate of Sanctuary. Within seconds Reilly heard a shot fired and the sound seemed to come from his friend's house. He turned to see Cousins stagger out into the road clutching his stomach. Reilly quickly raised the alarm and neighbours along with Dr Anglim were soon on the scene. The doctor would testify at the inquest on 28 March that he reached the scene within five minutes and 'found a man lying on the road wounded'. He said that the injured man spoke to him and complained of pain. A car was acquired from Mister White – they were quite rare at that time – to take the injured man to hospital. Unfortunately he died en route.

Gardaí arrived on the scene and intensive investigations ensued. They discovered a hole cut in the hedge on the passage to the house which would have allowed the killer to lie concealed before making the attack. The person identified as having been seen making that cut was Jane O'Brien but there was neither a weapon nor an obvious motive. The former was provided during a search of the house when a shotgun was discovered between the mattresses of O'Brien's bed. The motive that emerged centred on the probability of John Cousins getting married. Should that happen the tenure of O'Brien and her son would have been at risk. She was arrested and conveyed to the Garda station in Wexford, then situated in George's Street. At a special sitting of the court in Wexford she was formally charged with murder. A later preliminary hearing attracted large crowds to the courthouse, with many unable to gain entry and instead standing outside to glimpse the accused. After three hours and many witnesses she was sent forward for trial in the Central Criminal Court in Dublin.

At that trial Sergeant Patrick Hanley described the search of the house where he was accompanied by Chief Superintendent McCarthy and Superintendent O'Halloran. He stated that the chief superintendent addressed the accused in the bedroom saying, 'I know the gun is here. Please hand it over.' O'Brien pointed to the bed. The mattress was raised and a single-barrel shotgun was found. He stated that there were four mattresses on the bed and the weapon was between them. The gun smelled of gunpowder, indicating that it had been fired recently.

Richard Kelly, who had land adjoining Sanctuary, gave evidence of seeing a hole cut in the hedge on 27 March. Annie Maguire, who was engaged to the deceased and was waiting to marry after twelve months' mourning her father, also gave evidence. She said that she had recently received numerous anonymous postcards. No mention was made of the contents but she revealed that on one occasion she had met Jane O'Brien in the local post office when the accused said, 'I had better run out for fear Nan would blame me for sending postcards'. The witness had never mentioned postcards to O'Brien before this. She stated that both she and John considered the accused to be the sender of the postcards. Other witnesses included Dr Michael O'Brien, surgeon at Wexford County Hospital; George Cooke, gun expert, North Main Street, Wexford; and Commandant Daniel Stapleton, Ordnance Inspector, Islandbridge Barracks.

Bridget Quinn, a wardress at Waterford Prison, and Captain Arthur Quirke, a handwriting expert, gave evidence that the handwriting on the postcards matched that in O'Brien's diary.

Despite protest from the counsel for the accused, the judge allowed a statement made by Jane O'Brien at Wexford Garda Barracks on Monday 28 March be read to the court:

> I am Mrs Jane O'Brien. I reside in Sanctuary, Killinick in the house of my brother William Cousins who died about three months ago. I am twelve years here last May. Previous to my coming here I lived at Yoletown. My husband Andrew O'Brien lived with me then. At that time he was working on the railway, principally at Rosslare Harbour. About five years ago he went away to Scotland and subsequently he went to England. I last saw my husband three years next July ago. I had only one child, John, who is still with me here. The deceased, John Cousins, was my nephew. After his mother died twelve years ago John and his father begged me to come and live with them, and that I could do whatever I liked. They said for the whole family to come that the house was big enough and that we would all be happy together.

Later in the statement she said that she knew John Cousins would inherit the house and 5 or 6 acres and, before agreeing to live there, she spoke to him saying, 'Now, John, in years to come you might be getting married and I could go on the road'. She said that he replied, 'As long as you stay I'll never think of a woman and never marry'.

After summing up, the jury retired at 5.30 p.m. but because the counsel for the defence objected to some issues they were recalled for the judge to clarify matters. They retired again at 6.50 p.m. They returned a verdict of guilty but recommended mercy, taking into account the age and gender of the accused. In keeping with the law, the judge donned the black cap and sentenced Jane O'Brien to death with the date of 30 June set. He agreed to forward the recommendation of the jury to the proper quarter.

The Minister for Justice granted a reprieve from death after an unsuccessful appeal when the execution date was reset for 28 July.

DEATH IN TAGHMON

James Redmond lived in a caravan at Tottenham Green in Taghmon, County Wexford, in 1937. He was aged 45 years and his life ended violently in that caravan at some point between 11 and 25 January in that year.

The body was discovered by his sister Mary on 25 January. At an inquest held, as was usual in those days, at a house near the site of death, she recalled having gone to the caravan a number of times in recent days but, finding the door locked and his bicycle missing, she assumed he had gone away for a while. On the 25th she had investigated further in the area surrounding the caravan and 'saw a dark object' which turned out to be her brother. She alerted her other brother Patrick who she met with his daughter tending some sheep. She 'whispered the news to him as she did not want to frighten the little girl'. Patrick stated that 'he was present when the guards took the body out of the gripe on Monday evening. He recognised that it was the body of his brother.' It was obvious that he had died a violent death. James was described as a quiet man who kept very much to his own company. He was a labourer but had worked in England and in Canada before returning to Taghmon in the early 1930s. It appears that he had lived a frugal life during his travels and local belief was that he had saved a considerable 'nest egg' in that time. Some estimates put the sum at £300, a considerable amount in those days.

Following the grim discovery of Redmond's body, suspicion fell on John Hornick, a married man with three children also residing in Taghmon on what was described as a 'substantial farm'. The trail to Hornick started on discovering an Ulster Bank envelope in Redmond's caravan that should have contained a deposit slip which was missing, indicating robbery as a motive. The victim's bicycle was also missing and it was later discovered concealed on Hornick's property. Hornick had been known to have money problems but suddenly he 'began to be suspiciously free with money'. He paid off outstanding debts and started spending on cattle, a mare, pigs and furniture. It emerged during the investigation that he had tried unsuccessfully to cash the deposit receipt in New Ross. He then went to Dún Laoghaire where he got £280 from the bank by forging Redmond's signature.

During March of that year a total of eighty-four witnesses were deposed in Wexford and New Ross with the accused being sent for trial at the Central Criminal Court. Upwards of 100 witnesses would testify for the prosecution at the trial. These included Raymond Corish, auctioneer; Samuel Willis, ticket collector on the Dublin–Wexford train; Patrick McGuinness, booking clerk for New Ross railway station; Hugh Maguire, Ulster Bank Wexford and numerous neighbours from the Taghmon region. Much of their evidence was circumstantial, clearly establishing his movements before and after the murder. The defence offered no witnesses and Hornick did not testify. On day four of the trial, closing arguments were made. The judged instructed the jury and, within a short time, a guilty verdict was returned. The accused was sentenced to be executed on 5 May.

SWEET SHOP SLAYING

Sometime late on the night of 8 March 1958 William Hannan was murdered in his small shop in Harper's Lane, known to locals as Cinema Lane, by person or persons who have never been identified to this day. Ironically the killers were actually seen making their getaway and Gardaí were on the scene within minutes but to no avail.

The small sweet shop called The Dainty was only yards from Wexford's Main Street and almost opposite a busy Palace Cinema whose patrons he stayed open late to serve.

At first it was thought that the victim might have fallen from a ladder but it was later established that he had sustained numerous blows. He was not killed outright and was attended to at the scene but, unfortunately, he was to pass away next morning without being able to assist the investigation.

As well as tending his sweet shop, Mr Hannan indulged in a hobby of printing on a hand press in a small back room off the shop. In recent years he had reprinted hundreds of copies of 'Saint Columcille's Prophecies' which he sold widely to addresses in Ireland, England and the United States. It was thought that robbery was the initial motive but the thieves must have panicked because coins valued up to £3 were found on the floor and £276 on his person.

The victim was discovered by some men playing cards in a nearby house who heard moaning sounds and possible scuffling at about 10.45 p.m. William Scanlon went to investigate and, finding The Dainty in darkness, he banged on the door. There was still moaning to be heard so, along others who had arrived on the scene, he raised the alarm and Garda Martin Bond arrived. He gained entry by breaking a pane of glass in the door and found the victim.

It was later considered that the ladder which people had initially thought Mr Hannan had fallen from, was in fact the getaway route. It was surmised that the culprits made their way out of the skylight on hearing the alarm being raised. They then proceeded over the roof tops and descended into Henrietta Street, which runs parallel to Harper's Lane. This proved providential for the killers.

A short time earlier a car had been accidentally driven into the Crescent Quay and attracted a very large crowd to witness the efforts to remove it. The criminals had simply to blend into the crowd and disappear. Gardaí appealed for information on two men aged about 22 years who had left Wexford on the Monday after the murder. Their descriptions were circulated throughout the British Isles but without success.

When Gardaí searched The Dainty they found two short stories written by Mister Hannan. One entitled 'The Legacy' featured a case about a man murdered for his money.

There is an unrelated apocryphal story told in Wexford of a detective shooting a young man as he made his way over some rooftops. The man's mother was said to have cursed the shooter and legend has it that within weeks his 'trigger finger' had decayed.

THE £10 BOX OF MATCHES

There was an interesting case reported from Wexford District Court in March 1942. Mrs K. Whitty and Miss Margaret Bailey were in court because of the price charged for a box of matches. T.J. Kelly, State solicitor, prosecuted and the defence was led by Mr L. Kirwan.

Stephen McMahon, a town councillor, stated in the witness box that, on 24 October 1941, he had bought a box of matches in Mrs Whitty's shop where Margaret Bailey was the shop assistant. She charged him twopence for them. He requested a receipt which she furnished. He went immediately to the Garda barracks.

Sergeant Dempsey gave evidence that he went to the shop some time later with Mr McMahon to query the cost. Miss Bailey said that she had been told to charge twopence but Mrs Whitty denied having told her to charge that price.

Mr Kirwan for the defence said that the Price Order (which would determine prices) was not published until 12 November that year.

Mrs Whitty stated that on 19 October 1941 she had instructed her shop assistant to charge twopence for matches because there was a parade in town and she expected a rush of business. She said that she did not know then that the price had been fixed.

Miss Bailey did not serve in the shop between that date and 24 October when Mr McMahon came in and she had not had further instructions on the price. Therefore Mrs Whitty maintained that she had not instructed her to charge twopence on the day in question.

The justice asked Miss Bailey if she had done as she was told, to which she answered 'yes'. The justice said he was striking out the charge against her.

'But,' he continued, 'this is the first case of its kind in the county under the order and although the money is small the principle is big.' He noted that the purpose of the order was to protect the public and to curb the rapacity, greed and get-rich-quick methods of the profiteer and the racketeer. He said that the notices were published by the Department of Supplies and if people allowed themselves be cheated and swindled 'it was their own look out'. He pointed out that it was 'a good job for the defendant that it is the first case of its kind'. He also said that it was lucky that it involved neither food nor fuel because if it had a term of imprisonment would most likely have been imposed. He then fined Mrs Whitty £10 or three months in prison.

The gravity of such a crime came about because of the great shortages and rationing of goods in a time of war.

TITHES SEIZURE

A stack of wheat, which had been seized for tithes, was sold by auction at Ballymenane, parish of Ballindaggin, in 1836. After the wheat was bought, it was set on fire and destroyed. A public meeting was held to protest against this act of destruction. Mr James presided, and the chair was placed on the ashes of the wheat. The following, which was passed, is taken from the *Wexford Independent* of that time:

Proposed by Mr James Long, and seconded by Mr Moses Redmond resolved, that the barbarous burning of a stack of wheat, sold here on Monday, the 15th instant, for tithe, at the suit of John Rowe, the landlord, and purchased by Irvine, his agent, at whose instance the corn was consumed, has created in the public mind an extraordinary alarm, which we will endeavour to allay, and thus contribute to the preservation of that tranquillity and good order for which every part of this county is deservedly distinguished.

Sir James Power, then one of the members for the county, brought the subject before the House of Commons on several occasions. Both Mr Rowe and Mr Irvine strenuously denied, by letters in the newspapers, that they knew anything about the burning of the corn.

PROCLAMATIONS

The following is a selection of notices published in the newspapers and on posters. They give an interesting snapshot of the types of crimes and misdemeanours often lost in our history books, and shed a wonderful light on the everyday concerns. (Capitalisations are as they appeared.)

1735 For apprehending Nicholas POWER who made his escape out of the Gaol of Wexford.
1757 For forcibly carrying away Margaret KEARNEY, daughter of Anthony KEARNEY, of New Ross, County Wexford.
1779 For the persons who set fire to several houses in the County of Wexford, and who wrote threatening letters to Isaac CULLIMORE, and stabbed and wounded his cattle.
1786 For discovering, apprehending and prosecuting to conviction, the person or persons concerned in the burglary and felony committed in the house of Elizabeth HUGHES, of Ballymoney, in the County of Wexford and murdering her.

1801 For discovering and presenting to conviction the persons concerned in setting fire to the dwelling house of Thomas NEALE, of Ballinapiece, in the County of Wexford, and who murdered the said Thomas NEALE, and wounded his children.
1808 For discovering and apprehending the person who attacked William FLACK, a Corporal in the Wexford Militia, in the town of Carlow.
1816 For the discovery and apprehension of the persons concerned in the murder of Loftus FRIZELL, Esq., of Monamolin, in the County of Wexford.

INQUESTS IN 1841

(Note: 'Visitation from God' was a death where the cause was unknown.)

BANNON, James – on 18 December, at Coolcul, accidentally killed.
BOLTON, Joseph – on 6 November, at Oulart, murdered by a person or persons unknown.
BROWNE, John – on 21 December, at Wellingtonbridge, accidentally killed.
COBBETT, David – on 14 December, at the County Gaol, died of typhus fever.
DUGGAN, James – on 12 December, at Faith, Wexford, accidentally drowned.
DUGGAN, John – on 14 June, at Duncannon, accidentally smothered.
EBBS, Martha – on 24 December, at Gorey, died from the effects of a burning.
FENLONG, Mary – on 1 October, at St Leonard's, accidentally killed.
FITZSIMON, William – on 31 August, at Banogue [Bannow?], death from injuries received from some person of persons unknown.
FLEMING, Michael – on 23 October, at Gorey, died by visitation of God.
KELLY, Mary – on 24 March, at Ballygarrett, accidentally killed.
KINCHELLA, Daniel – on 10 March, at Inch, died by the visitation of God.

LACEY, Thomas – on 16 June, in Wexford, died of apoplexy.
LACEY, William – on 1 March, at Ballyregan, accidentally smothered.
LEARY, Michael – on 1 June, at Forrestalstown, accidentally killed.
LOTTO, John – on 28 September, at Courtown Harbour, accidentally drowned.
MAGUIRE, Thomas – on 9 July, at Enniscorthy, deceased was killed by Patrick Byrne.
MEYLER, Catherine – on 8 December, at Wexford, visitation of God.
MOORE, Daniel – on 23 April, at Ferrybank, death from intoxication.
NACEY, James – on 14 October, at Danescastle, died by visitation of God.
NEILL, Margaret – on 25 January, at Slippery Green, died from being accidentally burnt.
NEVILLE, Patrick – on 2 June, at Clonmines, murdered by a person or persons unknown.
PONDER, John – on 20 December, at Clonmore, accidentally killed.
POWER, Bridget – on 3 November, at Fethard, accidentally killed.
REDMOND, Elizabeth – on 19 June, at Ballymore, died of spasmodic asthma.
RODNEY, Mary Anne – on 18 March, at Wexford, accidentally burnt.
SINNOTT, Mary – on 16 June, at the County Gaol, died of apoplexy.
STAFFORD, James – on 16 August, at Castlebridge, accidentally killed.
TOPHAM, Catherine – on 17 May, at Kiltealy, found drowned.
WADE, Nancy – on 23 June, at Boderin, died by visitation of God.
WHITE, Mary – on 30 July, at Ballyconger, died by visitation of God.
WHITE, Mary – on 3 September, at Ardamine, death was caused by self-destruction.
WICKAM, Mathew – on 15 March, at Bishop's Water, died of apoplexy.

(Source: The British Parliamentary Papers on Ireland.)

WEXFORD GAOL REGISTER

1894

Bolger, Mary; 36, Enniscorthy – Indecent Behaviour; 7 days
Nugent, Margaret; 36, Duncormick – Drunkenness; 7 days
Nugent, Joseph; 29, Duncormick – Drunkenness; 7 days
Byrne, Patrick; 43, Wexford – Drunkenness; 48 hours
Byrne, Patrick; 50, New Ross – Drunkenness; 1 week
Jordan, Michael; 23, Enniscorthy – Assault; 14 days
Jordan, John; 25, Enniscorthy – Drunkenness & Disorderly; 1 month
Barron, Patrick; 32, Duncormick – Steal or trying to steal oats and Indian corn; 2 months
Redmond, James; 60, Kilcormick (near Enniscorthy) – Larceny of Saw; 1 month
Stamp, Jasper; 41, Wexford – Drunkenness; 48 hours
Lacy, Denis; 55, Vinegar Hill – Trespass; 7 days
Walsh, Mary; 66, Enniscorthy – Indecent Behaviour; 7 days
Whitty, Bridget; 47, Wexford – Drunkenness; 48 hours
Sweeney, Catherine; 48, New Ross – Drunkenness; 1 month
Clarke, James; 28, Wexford – Drunk & Quarrelsome; Remand
Murphy, Hannah; 18, Wexford – Riotous; 7 days
Dunbar, Mary; 45, Enniscorthy – Vagrancy; 14 days
Allen, Margaret; 49, Gorey – Larceny of Mutton; 3 months
Lyons, Mary; 18, Gorey – Breaking glass; 14 days

1895

Power Ann; 16, New Ross – Assault; 1 week
Mythan William; 24, Enniscorthy – Drunkenness; 7 days
Sinnott Patrick; 24, Wexford – Drunkenness; 1 month
Cogley Aiden; 40, Enniscorthy – Assault on wife; Remand
Bishop Richard; 20, Wexford – Drunkenness; 14 days

8

MUSICAL COUNTY

County Wexford basks in a wonderful musical tradition and this is reflected in the ballads that permeated the lives of our forefathers. In pre-radio and television days these were used to disseminate news, recall legends and to entertain. These often include the sea shanties and mournful, or sometimes humorous, songs associated with the maritime heritage. Farther Joseph Ranson's *Songs of the Wexford Coast*, first published in 1948 is one of the best-known collections.

In these ballads – sung in homes, pubs and any social gatherings – the people of the county recalled ships like *Alfred D. Snow*, lost in 1850, as well as other ships, such as *Vivandeer*, *Eliza* and *Mexico*, the subject of the Fethard Disaster of 1914. *Leinster* which was a mail boat torpedoed in 1918 , is also remembered as is *St Patrick*, a mail boat bombed in 1941.

The ballads commemorated Captain Coulson, who repulsed a pirate gang and saved 362 passenger lives; Jack (now recalled as John) Barry, who was appointed commodore of the US Navy, as well his contemporary Paul Jones, another American commander.

There were also songs of emigration like 'The Kilrane Boys' with lines such as:

> My darling boys what is the cause or reason you must go
> To leave your native country for a shore you do not know.

This song was written by a national school teacher from The Bing in Kilrane on the centenary of the emigration that had occurred in 1844. As part of those celebrations the actual cart used to ferry the boys to the ship was drawn in procession through the village.

The emigrants had departed not for the usual United States of America but rather to Buenos Aires in Argentina.

Not all Wexford ballads are exclusively from Wexford or enjoyed here. 'The Wreck of the Mary Jane' was popular in Dublin as well as Wexford:

> The Mary Jane was a one-mast ship,
> She was built in the 'town' of Taghmon,
> She carried a crew of one hundred and two,
> With a cargo of farmer's dung.
> The mate was a great navigator
> And his nose was as red as a tart,
> He belonged to the Wexford Militia
> And he knew every pub on the chart.

Dublin-born Patrick J. McCall (1861–1919) was the son of a Wexford mother and a Carlow father. His inspiring and often patriotic ballads include 'Sailing in the Lowlands Low', recalling the smuggling adventures of Wexfordmen during the eighteenth century:

> Dunmore we quitted, Michaelmas gone by;
> Cowhides and wool and live cargo,
> Twenty young Wild Geese ready-fledged to fly,
> Sailing for the Lowlands Low.
> Pray, holy Brendan, Turk nor Algerine,
> Dutchman nor Saxon may sink us
> We'll bring Geneva, Rack and Rhenish wine
> Safely from the Lowlands Low.

'The Wexford Massacre' recalls Oliver Cromwell who, in 1649, demanded the unconditional surrender of the town. Colonel David Sinnott refused but, after several days of negotiation and possible bribery, Stafford, the captain of Wexford Castle, allegedly threw open the town gates and a massacre is said to have ensued.

The short-lived rebellion of 1798 inspired ballads in every generation. We still hear 'Boolavogue'; 'Kelly from Killanne'; 'The Boys of Wexford'; 'At Monaseed in Sweet Co. Wexford'; 'The Croppy Boy'; 'Bagenal Harvey's Farewell';

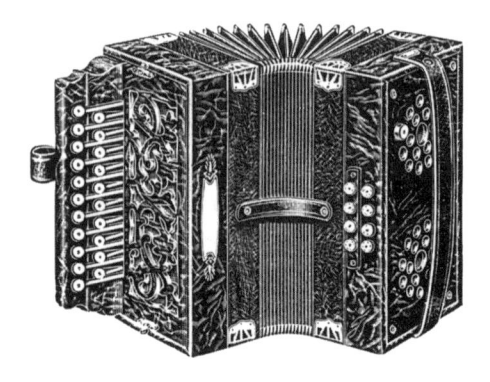

'The Wexford Insurgent'; 'The Men of '98'; 'The Battle of Vinegar Hill'; 'The Wexford Pikeman'; and 'The Heroine of Ross' to greater and lesser extent at wakes, weddings and funerals.

'The Boys of Wexford', written by Robert Dwyer-Joyce, is often referred to as the Wexfordmen's national anthem. What most of those belting it out in pubs and taverns often fail to notice, because they seldom reach the later verses, is that in many ways it is an anti-drinking song, blaming drink in part for the failure of the Rising.

The Wexford 1798 ballad is of course 'Boolavogue', first published in January 1898, the centenary year of the '98 rebellion.

A song of many versions is 'The Croppy Boy', recalling how the yeomanry, on sacking a Wexford chapel close to the County Waterford border, had one of their soldiers impersonate a priest in the confessional. On hearing the young man's story they seized the unfortunate youth and dragged him along to Geneva Barracks where he was shot without mercy.

> Good people all, who may pass by,
> Breathe a prayer and a sigh for the Croppy Boy.

Like words and expressions, there are controversies as to whether a ballad is exclusive to any area. One of these is 'The Verdant Braes of Screen' which, unfortunately, appears to be one we cannot claim, despite our parish of that name. One would contend, however, that the beautiful 'Bantry Girl's Lament' is one of ours, referring to the Barony of Bantry rather than the County Cork town.

Place names, people and events are enshrined in our ballad lore in the older songs but also in recently written and recorded tracks, including: 'Sweet Slaneyside'; 'Slaney Far Away'; 'Carrig River'; 'Beauties of Johnstown Castle' 'Sweet Tara Cove'; 'Good Old Monageer' and 'The Strawberry Fair'. 'The Village Curs' recalled the antics that 'young lads' got up to in days long past, like 'unyoking asses, cobs and ponies' while people were at Mass.

Folk-singer Burl Ives commented in the introduction to his book, *Irish Songs and Ballads*: 'To know these songs is to realise anew the genius of the Irish mind – that it can express troubles and bitterness, not only in fine martial strains, but also with such admirable humour, in the same breath.'

The year 1951 witnessed the beginning of a major cultural event in Wexford, the Wexford Festival Opera. The brainchild of Dr Tom Walsh, Dr Des Ffrench, Eugene McCarthy and Seamus Dwyer began at the Theatre Royal in that year. The first production was *The Rose of Castile* by Balfe, who, by coincidence, had lived for a time in Wexford. The first festival was opened by Lord Longford, whose touring theatre group had often played at the Theatre Royal. The opera festival has grown into a top-class international event with fringe events embracing all forms of the arts. The policy of staging top-quality, but often neglected, operas proved a winner. One of the benefits of this festival has been the blossoming of latent artistic talents in Wexford people in all spheres.

County Wexford has rested on its traditional or operatic laurels in recent years. As the 'ballad boom' and the 'rock and roll years' emerged the county was still to the fore.

George Hess was known locally as Gunner Hess, probably, like so many nicknames, because of his father's naval experience. In Ireland he played for a time with the Clipper Carlton Showband as well as The Premier Aces and the local Lowney Band before spreading his wings. In the United Kingdom he used the stage name Jim Gunner and was based, like so many musicians of that era, in Liverpool. He recorded in 1960 on the Decca label that had rejected The Beatles. The Wexford-born guitarist is believed to have been our first native to enter the British charts. Most people probably never heard the song 'Hooley Jump' by Jim Gunner & the Echoes but it did enter the Top 100.

In the 1960s Wexford was not bypassed in the folk boom. It embraced the revival of this tradition with gusto and held a number of Ballad Festivals to complement the sessions taking place in The Long Room, White's Barn and other venues. One of the groups to emerge from one of those Ballad Festival competitions was The Johnstons who went on to worldwide fame and from which Paul Brady emerged as a solo artist. There is a story that two groups were runners-up in one such competition. One was called The Emmets and the other Spiceland. Having failed to clinch a title, they merged as Emmet Spiceland and had a few top hits like 'Mary From Dunloe' and 'Bunclody'.

There was another festival back in the 1970s. Wexford Festival of Living Music was an ambitious undertaking but even the title got some backs up as they saw it as a slight on opera, inferring that it wasn't living music. In March 1971, the first Wexford Festival of Living Music was staged by Tapestry Theatre, a group of young people aiming to put Wexford on the arts map. On that St Patrick's week their first series of events kicked off, with bookings reported as coming in from Britain, Holland and the United States, and hotels and guesthouses appearing delighted with the prospects.

The Theatre Royal was the venue for two concerts. The first featured Danny Doyle, The Johnstons and The Strawbs. Another had The Chieftains as one of the acts. In the Abbey Cinema there was live music from Southern Comfort and Curved Air on one night and Dr Strangely Strange and Fairport Convention on a later date. Meanwhile, in Dun Mhuire Mellow Candle, Tír na nÓg and Principal Edwards Magic Theatre filled the bill.

The festival featured a John McCormack record recital and museum at Whites Hotel. *Murder in the Cathedral* was staged in St Iberius' church and poets like Peter Fallon and Brendan Kennelly gave readings. The Ulster Youth Orchestra performed and Monica Carr provided a lecture and 'cook-in' at the Talbot Hotel.

The following year, despite financial problems, Tapestry Theatre was again attracting top acts of the day to Wexford. In the Abbey, The Chieftains and Shades of McMurrough provided the entertainment. At Dun Mhuire, Horslips and Supply Demand and Curve were the featured artistes. The final concert had Planxty and East of Eden in the Abbey, where there were reports of revellers dancing on the balcony wall. Each concert cost 50p admission. In addition, late-night film shows for 20p each featured Easy Rider, Yellow Submarine and Let It Be.

Local headlines a week later were:

> 'Living Music Festival Slammed'
> 'It Mustn't Happen Again'
> 'Wexford Recovers from Hippy Invasion'

There was public outrage and indignation. Reports of young people sleeping together in doorways, the old sawmill at The Crescent being dubbed a 'Hippy Hostel' and some window breaking by an unruly element saw recriminations and counter claims In the end, however, Living Music was killed in its infancy.

One Wexfordian who played with the Horslips in that latter festival would go on to be one of the most influential, if perhaps underestimated, musical influences in Ireland. He is Declan Sinnott. He started out, like all good musicians, with his own group in Wexford, influenced no doubt by the growing music industry worldwide. He graduated to the national scene with bands like Horslips and Moving Hearts. But it was as a musical director and record producer that Sinnott probably made most impact. His many years with Mary Black helped to shape her international career. He was her accompanist for over a decade, impressing all who witnessed his superb guitar playing. In more recent years he has emerged from the shadows, not only releasing his own album but as a sort of double act with Christy Moore, playing sell-out concerts throughout the British Isles.

With such a rich and diverse musical history, who can imagine what our musical future holds?

PERSONAL REFLECTIONS ON THE FESTIVAL OPERA

This is a personal look back on Wexford Festival Opera. Not being overly age-sensitive I will admit that I grew up with the festival. Actually, I suppose, like many if not most residents of Wexford,

I grew up parallel to the opera festival. Granted there were and are opera aficionados, buffs and stars in our midst, but I think for most of us the happenings within the hallowed walls of the old Theatre Royal held little attraction. Not that we were musical morons; most families had an abiding interest in music but it was more likely 'The Old Bog Road', 'Noreen Bawn' or that other beacon of Wexford musical talent 'Carrig River' that was heard in sitting rooms, wakes and weddings from my Aunt Peggy or Uncle Peter.

Festival for us was the Guinness Clock, fireworks, Kelly's window, a bottle of minerals and odd-looking characters strolling the Main Street.

The Guinness Clock, which we thought was unique, and sometimes even more mistakenly, solely brought out for Wexford, was one of a set that toured the United Kingdom. But we loved it when it arrived in Redmond Place every October. We stood clutching the hands of Ma and Da as the quarter hour ticked closer and the show began with bells and whistles and whirling figures. This lasted a few minutes and then was replaced with whimpers and whines as we want to wait for the next 'show'.

Fireworks were *the* item of the opening night of festival. Today young people are a bit blasé about them. They see huge displays on television in HD and they even have their own displays for parties. Back in the 1950s no one could use fireworks without a licence and Wexford was quite unique in having its display.

In those early years the opening ceremony was not overrun with politicians as guest speakers and 'festival openers'. I recall Val Doonican doing the honours one year. Another it was the lad from down in Bargy Castle, Chris DeBurgh, then at the height of his fame. I recall that night in particular because it was in the days of the pirate radio stations and I won a signed copy of 'Spanish Train'. Another local celebrity doing the honours was Billy Roche. Looking back, I wonder when it slipped into being a showcase for ministers etc.

Opening night was famous for the Festival Window Displays. Okay, we still have them and some are very creative but all too often they are also professionally dressed. Back in the early days it was 'our people', shop workers we knew, coming up with ideas and following them through. Almost every shop on the Main Street took part and after the speeches and the fireworks there was a mass exodus from the quay or Church Lane on to the Main Street. Waves of people, from Grandas down to 'soft children' in tansads, flowed along in opposing directions, depending on where home was. Maybe because bread and cakes lent themselves to displays, the crowds ended up five- or maybe ten-deep around Kelly's Bakery. It wasn't just the physical display that attracted people, there was always humorous or even satirical themes to the windows, based on the news events of the time.

The next attraction of Opening Night was a few chips and a bottle of minerals. This was one of the few times that whole families would parade the Main Street and the Das pockets were open wide as the children were treated. It was a truly magical night.

For most of us that was *the* Festival – one brilliant night.

There were other things we noticed as we got older. In those days, when television was only arriving and holidays meant Rosslare Strand in a hut or caravan, we were fascinated by the characters who erupted on to our streets from September onwards. Men in big coats with fur collars and maybe even fur hats, ladies in unusual dresses and capes, and all speaking in languages we had never heard before. Young people today, exposed to all manner of foreign travel, foreign friends and wall-to-wall television, will never understand the impact of those visitors. When the performances began the other exotic creatures arrived; the audiences in their evening dress, furs, hats and other outfits were a performance in themselves as they hurried from White's, The Talbot or The County Hotel to the shows each night. On the night of The Opera Train we got a sort of fashion parade as the band met the special train from Dublin and the visitors walked to the Theatre Royal.

Another festival attraction that I always regret missing was The Festival Forum. This was a sort of prototype *Late Late Show* where a panel of experts, raconteurs and entertainers were brought together in the Palace Cinema for a night of lively debate and controversy. Speakers included Sir Compton McKenzie, Lord Longford and Ulick O'Connor.

In later years I became more involved as a volunteer and, as well as seeing a fascinating art form up close, met another wave of colourful characters ranging from Charlie Fitz, who resided in his mobile home as he reported on the operas for the *Belfast Telegraph*, through correspondents from *The Sunday Times* and *Observer*, directors of Santa Fe Opera and a lady who felt that Wexford Festival Opera and the town would afford an excellent setting for a murder mystery.

The art exhibitions were less numerous and the festival tours less ambitious but we had lectures on topics ranging from opera production to gardening to travelling in America.

9

WORKING WEXFORD

INDUSTRY AND LABOUR IN THE 1800S

In the middle of the nineteenth century those gathering statistics often referred to what we know as trades as 'mechanics' and, in one such report, we find 'mechanics such as masons and carpenters are paid 2 shillings sixpence a day without support and town labourers principally those engaged in the building trade are paid from 10 pennies to one shilling a day'. The farm labourer got between 2s 6d and 3s 6d a week. He often got use of a patch of land to grow potatoes for which he repaid the farmer in extra labour.

In Wexford in the 1840s through into the 1850s the main source of employment was on the developing quays. With the exception of shipbuilding which in those years employed about thirty carpenters, there were no other major manufacturing industries.

Mr Donnelly owned a small foundry employed a few men and Peter Murphy had a millwright business at Crescent Quay. Mr Landers had a coach-building firm on the quay. This was a time prior to the railway and transport was by sea or coach.

The shipping trade facilitated a major malting trade in Wexford. One maltster named John Barrington 'turned out 60,000 barrels in a season'. Others involved in the trade in the mid-nineteenth century included Patrick Breen of a Castlebridge family, Richard Walsh, Robert Stafford and William Whitty.

Between the malting and general commercial trade of the port, the principal owners were Devereux, Allen and Gaffney. The incoming trade to Wexford Port had increased greatly in the Famine years, with yellow corn being imported from the Danube ports. Devereux and Allen had extra ships built in that period to cope with the trade.

Around 1870 there were seventy sailing vessels owned by people of the town and hinterland.

BACON CURING BUSINESS

During the European wars of the late eighteenth and early nineteenth centuries, Kough's of New Ross were government contractors supplying cured bacon and beef for the British army and navy. The family firm had one of their number stationed as far away as Newfoundland as an agent.

The trade was well paid and the company's employees, known as 'salters', resided together in an area of New Ross extending down Follyhouse Lane and Fairgate to Goat Hill and the Royal Hotel. It is reported that on Sundays these employees strode about the town gaudily dressed with buckles on shoes and knees.

By 1834 the bacon factory was located on The Quay in New Ross and had a considerable trade established with London and the north of England. The brand is said to have held 'first place' in the London market. Around this time, tastes were changing from the traditional 'heavy salted' to 'mild cured' bacon and Kough & Son adapted successfully to the new process.

In the 1800s the product was sent by boat on the Barrow to Waterford for shipment to England. The factory closed in the early 1880s only to reopen in 1888 under Samuel Kough, curing 500 pigs per week to meet demand in Waterford and Leinster. The family sold the factory to David Murphy, a draper, and Martin Doherty, and under their management it continued until 1907.

LABOUR ORGANISES

Before the American trend for acronyms took hold with SIPTU and NALGO, we had unions whose names told the story of the workers without the aid of a dictionary.

Among the organisations sending delegates to the councils of trade union meetings back in the earlier decades of this century was the Amalgamated Society of House and Ship Painters. The dual occupation probably indicates that the number of ships to be painted in Ireland at the time was on the decline.

The Sailors and Firemen's Union causes some confusion in the modern mind. People might ask how seafarers and those who put out fires would belong to the same union. This is easily explained by the changed meaning of words over the years. The firemen in this union were not firefighters but those who kept the fires going, in the boilers and engine-rooms of sea-going vessels.

The printers of the last century used the title 'Typographical Society', which somehow seems very much more important and professional than a mere union. This group also had, and I believe maintain to the present day, a rather mysterious organisational system. Instead of branches they have chapels. And what would in other groups be called a shop steward is for the printers the 'Father of the Chapel'.

One of the longest titles of a union to be found in the labour world of 1917 must have been the Incorporated Guild of Stone and Brick Layers. Such a grandiose title harks back to medieval times, when guilds were among the first labour organisations. However, in those earlier centuries, they were usually concerned with self-employed people, since this is what the majority of artisans were.

It was these guilds who originated the famous Mystery Plays of that period, which are still performed in places like York to this day. The guilds usually used the plays, based on religious themes, to portray members of their particular occupation in the best light. For instance, a carpenters guild would probably use the Nativity as a theme with St Joseph as a carpenter having a major role.

Contrary to popular belief, trade unions and organised labour were not confined to the urban areas. Even before towns formed their trades council, farm labourers had their Trade and Labour Leagues who fought for better conditions and wages for agricultural labourers. It was the generous fundraising by such rural bodies that helped ward off starvation for men trying to establish trade unions in the towns and cities of the first decades of this century.

The National Union of Life Insurance Agents was another of the groups of workers listed in Ireland over eighty years ago, along with the Postmen's Federation and the Sawyers Union. The existence of a sawyers union indicates the abundance of local sawmills in provincial towns of the day. Similarly, a branch of the Railwaymen's Union shows that a large number of people must have been employed in rail transportation.

In Wexford in 1917 a Trades and Labour Council was established to 'Promote the moral and social elevation of the operative classes. To give increased efficiency to labour organisations. To consider all questions affecting the interests of labour and to encourage local and Irish industry.'

At that time the councils tackled issues such as work being sent outside the town or country for completion, profiteering among shopkeepers, lack of surgeons in the local infirmaries and illegal rent increases by landlords.

Apart from looking for better conditions for workers and negotiating for wage increases, trade unions have continued to tackle wider social problems. They give support to workers in developing countries and to Irish workers trying to improve the lot of those in these countries.

Sadly, the ship painters, the firemen and other occupations have gone, taking not only the jobs but the inspired titles of their organisations, leaving us with the acronyms which few people can connect with particular occupations and which will be of little use to those researching the trades of the late twentieth century.

TOBACCO IN COUNTY WEXFORD

More associated with the southern states of the United States of America, we are often surprised to hear of a tobacco-growing industry on our doorstep. In 1828 upwards of 1,000 acres of tobacco was grown in County Wexford, mainly by small cottiers. Western Niaca, usually used as a pipe tobacco, was most popular because its heavy leaf gave good returns.

Beds made of horse dung, clay and sand, with maybe a little sulphur or potash added were used to germinate the seeds. The young tobacco plants were left in these 'hot beds' until they were ready to be planted out in the field. They were sheltered from the wind by Jerusalem artichokes. The plants usually grew to about 3ft in height.

Six to eight weeks after topping, the tobacco was sufficiently ripe to harvest. Curing then took place in the tobacco shed. Up to twenty women worked in each shed, hanging leaves at different levels. In Broadway the leaves were dried by steam, but the steam was too expensive to maintain so the leaves were then dried by coke fires.

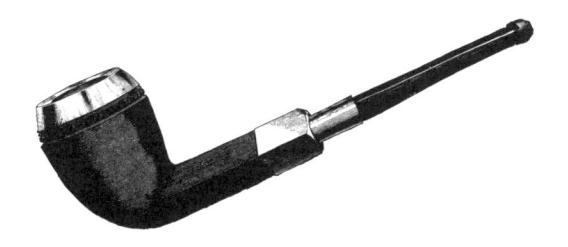

The Imperial Company bought the tobacco from the farmers, grading it into first, second and third class, and selling it accordingly.

Unfortunately, its success was to cause problems. English trade with the tobacco-growing states of America was also being injured and legislative restrictions were imposed by an Act of Parliament in 1831. In 1907, an Act repealing all the statutes prohibiting the cultivation of tobacco in Ireland was passed and a year later a Tobacco Growing Society was formed in County Wexford.

Although profits were being made, there was still a duty on tobacco-growing. By 1931 a Mr Devereux recalled making £240 an acre profit. In 1933 the Irish Government, in its efforts to boost home industries, removed the duty on the growing of tobacco. Then the government realised that if the acreage under tobacco was extended it would reduce imports of tobacco from England and America – the government would lose an important source of revenue in taxing such imports. Their answer was to restrict cultivation to a less robust plant and to control the price of tobacco. Within a few years many farmers gave up cultivating tobacco. Now the industry is gone.

WEXFORD INDUSTRIES IN 1937

Aonach Carman, or the Wexford Fair, was held in 1937 and, looking at some of the companies who took part, we are reminded of the industrious nature of the county in that period.

From the years prior to the Great Famine, the tanning business of T. Jones & Co. had flourished in New Ross. It had started with the production of harness leather but, by 1937 (as The New Ross Tanning Industry), it was its sole leather that had nationwide sales. Also in New Ross, Cherry's Brewery was producing beer, ales and minerals. It too was over a century in business by the 1930s and the produce sold well beyond the Leinster boundaries.

Graves & Company were described as one of the oldest established industrial enterprises in the Saorstat. Their hay sheds already dotted the country.

Particular pride was taken in a company manufacturing razor blades in Enniscorthy. Irish nationals had set it up in 1934 with purely

Irish capital and staffed entirely by Irish people. They produced 'Mac's Smile' and 'Garryowen' blades at a penny each. For those with more tender skin, they offered a range at twopence each. They boasted that they could supply all the razor blade needs of the Free State in one of the most modern plants in Europe.

10
COUNTY WEXFORD AND THE SEA

FETHARD LIFEBOAT DISASTER

On Friday, 20 February 1914 a Norwegian barque, *Mexico*, went aground off the Keeragh Islands, off the Wexford coast. Within a short time, the lifeboat from Fethard was at the scene. As it tried to approach the stricken vessel, it was lashed by a mighty wave and smashed to pieces.

Nine of the fourteen crew members were swept to their deaths as their companions and the men from the *Mexico* scrambled on to the nearby rocks. As these thirteen men clung to the rocks, the lifeboat from Kilmore attempted a rescue but was driven back by the fierce gale. The men spent a dark and stormy night on those inhospitable rocks.

Next day, the steam tug *Wexford* towed the lifeboat from Rosslare Fort to the scene to join the Dunmore East lifeboat in a rescue attempt. However, the storm was so strong that all boats had to shelter in harbour.

Throughout Sunday, they could only watch as their fellow seamen clung to the rocks in a storm too fierce for lifeboats to sail.

On Monday, another attempt was made. Still, the lifeboats could not approach the rocks, but two men, Bill Duggan and Jim Wickham of the Rosslare Fort lifeboat, took a dinghy and ferried the survivors, two at a time, from their ice-cold rocks.

The operation needed six trips in stormy seas to bring all to safety, but on the second of these, the dinghy was holed. For the remaining trips the sea was kept out by a loaf of bread wrapped in oilskins, plugged into the opening.

Many ballads were written of this sad disaster and heroic rescue, including the anonymous 'The Fethard Lifeboat Crew', containing the lines:

> The thunder roared, the lightning flashed, the seas like mountains ran,
> But onward 'mid that tempestuous storm the lifeboat proudly came.
> The signal which she flashed that night was the white o'er the green in view:
> The signal which a sailor reads: 'I will not abandon you.'
>
> As she neared the ill-fated Mexico, oh heavens what a shock,
> Their boat was dashed to pieces on the dreaded Keeragh Rock.
> Oh God what a sensation, to behold those heroes brave,
> Contending with the raging seas, their precious lives to save.
> The crew of the gallant *Mexico*, though terror stricken too,
> They rendered all assistance to the drowning lifeboat crew.
>
> Five of those gallant heroes were all that could be found.
> The other nine, by the Keeragh Rock, I'm sorry to say were drowned.
> May God have mercy upon their souls, who gave their noble lives,
> And heaven guard the helpless ones those heroes left behind.

HOSPITAL SHIP SUNK

Throughout the Second World War – or as it was called in Ireland, 'The Emergency' – thousands of men and women from County Wexford served with the Allied Forces. Until relatively recent times these people have often been forgotten in the writing of our history. Here is one such tale to remind us of the sacrifices they made.

A number of Irishmen lost their lives when the Great Western Railway's mail steamer *Saint David* was sunk off the Anzio beach in January 1944. On that date, along with *Saint Andrew* and MV *Leinster*, she was anchored off that beach head, taking off the wounded soldiers having been requisitioned to act as a hospital ship. The *Saint David* had earlier relieved casualties at Dunkirk, Normandy, Sicily and Salerno. All three ships were lit, as was required, with rows of green lights around the rails and well-illuminated Red Cross insignias at various points.

Despite this, a heavy bomber roared overhead. There was a huge explosion in number three hold and all the lights went out. One witness stated, 'I put on my life jacket and ran to my boat. I saw George Kelly from Waterford beside the boat but was never to see him again.' The ship gave a 'sickening lurch', her bows rose in the air and she went down stern first. Within five minutes of the bomb hitting, *Saint David* was gone. A boat that had not been cast off was capsized, tipping the sailors into the water. A young sailor named Breen, from Rosslare Harbour, recalled that he was in the water for some hours before being picked up and taken aboard MV *Leinster*, where he was diagnosed with a fractured skull. The number of men lost through the explosion or drowning was sixty-four, including Captain Owen who went down with his ship. Among the County Wexford casualties were Philip Maher from Duncannon and Quarter Master Todd from Rosslare Harbour.

SEA CAREER

In the middle of the twentieth century a career in the merchant marine was seen as a good option for the youth of County Wexford. As evidence of this we find Captain Freyne giving a lecture to pupils of Wexford Technical School entitled 'The Sea as a Career'. He was employed by the Department of Industry and Commerce but he stated that the content of his talk would reflect his own experiences as a seaman.

He noted that until Irish Shipping was launched there had been no foreign tonnage of note through Irish ports. This contrasted with the vibrant ports in Wexford and New Ross in times past but he was confident that the new company would prosper. In this way he stressed the future for new Irish sailors.

He explained that anyone intent on a sea career had to undergo an eye test. In carrying out such tests in Dublin he was surprised at how many people failed to note the importance of defective colour vision in such a career. He used lantern slides to test those present for colour blindness, which he estimated affected 5 per cent of the male population. Such colour blindness would be a major handicap in reading the various flag and light signals essential at sea.

He pointed out that would-be sailors needed to be physically fit. There could be no flat feet, varicose veins or hernias. He warned parents against thinking of a sea career as a 'cure' for tuberculosis.

Interestingly, he advised that, 'if a boy was fortunate to be born of such parents he should be kept at secondary school until he was seventeen and then he could go to technical school to sharpen himself up in manual matters'. It was not enough to train the mind. He needed manual skills like carpentry because 'as an officer he would have to give orders to a petty officer who was a carpenter'.

He recommended training on a 'cadet ship' and noted that this was quite expensive at £100 per year, but praised the training available. For those having to avail of the technical school education, he recommended learning carpentry, signalling, knotting and splicing. He also recommended elementary science and atmospheric refraction for navigation.

He said that when a boy went to sea 'his secular education should be complete' but he could continue to educate himself 'if he kept his books open in his spare time' on voyages. He could go back to technical college between voyages and 'anything puzzling him would be explained'.

After securing a second mate's certificate he would 'do eighteen months as a junior officer'. As third mate in 1944 he would be paid £17 per month plus a £10 war bonus. If he got a job as second mate the basic pay would be between £20 and £25, plus the war bonus. After securing a first mate certificate he would do another period before sitting an examination to become a master.

He stated that a career in 'the engine room had been almost exclusively left to the Scot'. However, he recommended the engineering side of seafaring as a career above those on deck.

In doing so he held out the prospect of retiring at 60 or even earlier on a reduced pension. They could then consider shore-bound careers as surveys, harbour masters or nautical assessors.

He said that having the Irish language was a distinct advantage. He had learned it in the West of Ireland and had also taken private lessons in French and Spanish, which proved very useful for foreign travel.

SPECTACULAR RESCUE

We are often indebted to the sparkling reportage of the journalists of local newspapers for records of events that, while exciting and heroic, would never make it into the history books. One such event occurred in Wexford Harbour in late summer of 1939.

That September a number of local cot owners organised one of the many regattas that formed the entertainment fabric of the port town of Wexford. With a heavy sea running and almost gale-force winds, the event proceeded with a very large crowd of spectators lining the quays.

Robert Roche of Saint Magdalen's Terrace and Jack Murphy from Fisher's Row were crewing the cot *Verdict* owned by Peter French of Fisher's Row in a race for 'first class cots' and were in the lead on the 'down run'. While manoeuvring their sails to change course for the return leg, the men were amazed to find the vessel 'sinking like a stone beneath their feet'. In an instant they were in the cold waters of the harbour and struggling to get clear of the mast and sails.

Like many sailors, Murphy was unable to swim. Roche somehow managed to get his companion on to his own back but that extra weight made it very difficult for him to keep afloat.

The *Alice D*, owned by Nicholas Fortune of Fisher's Row and manned by Michael Murphy of Gulbar Road and Thomas Pitman of Antelope Road, was in the process of passing the submerged craft, travelling at top speed. Michael leaned over the gunwale and grabbed the two men in imminent danger of drowning. *Alice D* never slackened its speed but somehow Michael, who was of rather slight build, managed, by some superhuman feat of strength, to haul both men on board. The crew 'hauled the sail aft' and continued the race.

People on the quay, who had seen *Verdict* go down and the men fall into the water, thought them lost and it was not until *Alice D* arrived into the quay that spectators were even aware of a daring high-speed rescue accomplished before their eyes. The boat had not only accomplished a life-saving exercise, it also shared the race honours.

Speaking later, Michael Murphy commented that it was the greatest of good fortune that *Alice D* had not been in the lead when the incident occurred because, even if they had witnessed the sinking, it would have been very difficult to bring the boat around in time to rescue the drowning men.

TITANIC CONNECTIONS

April 1912 will always be synonymous with one tragic incident, the sinking of the 'unsinkable' *Titanic*. We usually connect this great ship in Ireland with Belfast and then with Cobh as her last point of departure. But we forget the County Wexford connections.

Hugh McElroy, whose family came from Tullycanna, County Wexford, was the chief purser on the *Titanic*. He was also a close friend of Captain Smith and was photographed with him at the start of the voyage. It would have been McElroy who addressed the passengers when disaster struck, advising them to forget belongings and to proceed to the lifeboats. Born in Liverpool to parents originally from County Wexford, on his marriage to Barbara Ennis in 1910 he moved Harperstown, County Wexford. Prior to that Hugh had served on the *Britannic* during the Boer War, before taking up employment with the White Star Line at the turn of the twentieth century. McElroy went down with the ship but his body was recovered later. Reports in *The Echo* newspaper say that 'when his body was recovered he was wearing his ships uniform, a white jacket' and recovered on his person were the ship keys, ten pennies, 50 cents and a fountain pen. The newspaper report on 25 May 1912 stated, 'McElroy, 14 April on board RMS *Titanic*, Hugh, beloved husband of Barbara McElroy, Springwood, Wexford'.

Paddy McGough, an able seaman from Duncannon, survived the tragedy. He was quoted as saying 'No one was killed by the collision. I saw her back break and I heard an explosion.' He survived because he was one of the crew assigned to a lifeboat.

There are other intriguing references to Wexford-connected crew members. One of these was 'a sailor named Connors from Coolcotts' and Laurence Doyle, aged 27, whose address was listed as Southampton but believed to have been from Wexford.

There were two Wexford-born passengers on the *Titanic*. Elizabeth (Lizzie) Doyle, from Bree, was travelling to New York. The story goes that she decided to travel third class to save almost £3 on the fare. Ironically, this saving may have cost her life because 80 per cent of second-class passengers were saved, compared to 55 per cent of third class. She had lived in Chicago and had returned to Bree to nurse her widowed father through an illness, hence her presence on the *Titanic*. Her estate amounted to just £10 and legal papers referred to her as 'died at sea in an accident to the steamship *Titanic*'.

Lizzie was travelling with her cousin Robert Mernagh of Ballyleigh, Ballywilliam, County Wexford. He was returning to Chicago. He would leave an estate of £30. While not huge, the sums of money and the various travels across the Atlantic indicate that, although travelling third class, the people in question were in reasonable financial shape for 1912.

TUSKAR ROCK TRAGEDY

In March 1968 County Wexford became the focus of international attention for a very tragic reason. On the 24th of that month, late on a Sunday morning, the Aer Lingus Viscount flight EI712 called *Saint Phelim*, plunged mysteriously out of the sky near Tuskar Rock Lighthouse.

The 100-minute flight from Cork to London used one of the stalwarts of civil aviation of the period. The Viscount 803 had a seating capacity of sixty-five passengers. This particular plane was eleven years old but had only been in the Aer Lingus fleet for thirteen months. It had been certified air worthy just thirty-eight days before this doomed flight.

The captain on 24 March was Barney O'Brien, with first officer Paul Heffernan. One of the air hostesses on the flight was Anne Kelly. Although born in Dublin she had spent much of her youth in Wexford town, a few short miles from where her life would be cut tragically short.

The flight left Cork at 11.32 local time in fair weather. Twenty-five minutes later, Shannon Air Traffic Control instructed the captain to switch to London Airways to continue the journey. The *Saint Phelim*'s only contact with London Airways was an intercepted call – 'Echo India Alpha Oscar Mike with you' – at about noon Irish time. This designated the plane's registration number, EI-AOM, although the message was not the one normally used by Aer Lingus. But it was not a distress call. Eight seconds later they, along with the crew of another Aer Lingus plane, heard 'Twelve thousand feet, descending, spinning rapidly'. No more was heard but there is a ten-minute gap between the recorded time of the message and the timetable later established for eyewitness accounts of the plane. As usual with witnesses there was a wide range of reports, with the plane seen variously at Fethard-on-Sea, Saltee Islands, Hook Head and Greenore Point. Only two of the nineteen eyewitnesses reported seeing 'something go into the sea'. One was on the shore and another on a passing ship, the MV *Metric*. It was established that, around noon on that fateful day, people at some of those locations and at Broadway village, 3 miles inland, 'heard a bang' or 'a double clap like thunder from Tuskar Rock direction'.

But, according to Dermot Walsh in his book *Tragedy at Tuskar*, 'twenty-five miles west of where the plane dived into the sea, six witnesses saw an aeroplane, of whom four said it had "very red colour on part of the wings and tail" instead of the green and white livery of Aer Lingus'. This would feed a major theory regarding the fate of flight EI712.

From 12.25, Irish time, on 24 March, the sea around Tuskar Rock became a hive of search activity. Lifeboats from Rosslare Harbour, Kilmore Quay and Arklow rushed to the scene. British naval vessels HMS *Hardy*, HMS *Penelope* and *Invermoriston* steamed to the area. A Dove aircraft from the Irish Air Corps was joined by ten more planes from the United Kingdom within two hours.

No wreckage was found on that first day. The next day, with the Irish corvette LE *Macha* heading to the scene from Killybegs, the first six bodies were recovered by the frigate HMS *Hardy*. These were found about noon, twenty-four hours after the crash, 6 nautical miles north west of Tuskar Rock. Two more bodies were picked up by *Invermoriston* and one by the Rosslare Harbour lifeboat. According to Walsh there is much confusion in official records on these points, with denials that HMS *Hardy* ever landed bodies while *Invermoriston*, crewed by civilians and based in Pembroke, is acknowledged as entering Irish waters. The latter vessel is not recorded in departmental records as having been there.

Anne Kelly was one of the first casualties identified as the bodies were brought to Wexford Town where a make-shift mortuary was established. Unfortunately, the only bodies recovered were those taken ashore in those early days. Anne Kelly was buried in Crosstown Cemetery. Her funeral was a poignant occasion with her Aer Lingus colleagues forming a march guard of honour accompanying the hearse across Wexford Bridge.

On 26 March command passed to Irish naval sources with the LE *Cliona* joining the search, but, on 27 March, the two British Navy ships were officially requested to assist. The sea between Rosslare Harbour and Wales was thoroughly searched by boats of both navies, along with lifeboats, RAF planes, numerous small boats and a private plane owned by Wexford RNLI secretary John O'Loughlin. The search for survivors then changed to one of recovery.

Five days after the crash the State decided that, with no hope of survivors, they would take full charge and voluntary efforts ceased. On 30 March the British Navy mine-hunter HMS *Shoulton* and the mine-sweeper HMS *Clarbeston* arrived with diving experts in the immediate search area. Trawling activity was prohibited within a 6-mile radius of Tuskar Rock as sonar was used to search the depths. This continued through April and May, using underwater cameras, divers and electronic equipment.

On 5 June the Kilmore quay trawler *Glendalough*, skippered by Billy Bates, which had been recruited in the search, pulled the first pieces of fuselage from the water about 2 nautical miles from Tuskar Rock. Further pieces were recovered throughout that day.

The next day divers from HMS *Reclaim* reported that the mass of wreckage 'like a scrap yard' was located.

The recovery operation would extend over many months. It was hampered by tides and by miscalculation in trying to hoist the wreckage. The task was suspended a number of times due to the weather and eventually costs would play a factor in its continuation.

One of the main theories concerning the tragedy was that the *Saint Phelim* could have been struck by a projectile or a small plane. Every piece of debris raised by trawlers over the coming years reignited the debate about the so-called 'Rocket Alley', a wedge of airspace between Wales and the southern tip of Ireland that was the location of 'intensive operations and top secret exercises and manoeuvres' by the British military. There was speculation that flight EI712 had taken a 'shortcut' bringing it into the area. Theorists note that the British Navy was 'very quickly on the scene' and also that 'the spring tab of the plane, which could not float, was found 7 miles from the crash site'.

The crash is commemorated with a stone in Saint Ibar's Cemetery Crosstown where Anne Kelly is buried.

VESSEL IN DISTRESS

In January 1922 the SS *Active*, a Wexford-owned vessel, foundered off the Wexford coast. The steamer was the property of Mr P. Donovan and was on a voyage from Liverpool with a cargo of 262 tons of wheat, both in bags and bulk, bound for Davis' Mill in Enniscorthy.

As a result of a fierce storm, the vessel began to leak badly while she was about twenty hours out of Liverpool. Crew members later reported that, having left Liverpool, 'it came on to blow a hurricane from the north west'. The *Active* made poor headway in these conditions and was 'shipping water'. After twenty hours she was off the Blackwater Lightship and a crewman reported water in the stoke hold. Valiant efforts by the crew to stem the flow proved worthless.

Flares were lit and bed sacks set alight to try to attract attention. The *Lucifer* Lightship signalled a reply but no crew member was free to respond as the water was about to reach the furnaces. Then the engines gave in.

As she settled lower in the water, the crew took to the lifeboats. Two boats were lowered but one was smashed by heavy seas and the eight members in it had to scramble into the other boat. By now *Active* was settled to the gunwales and some waves 'broke clean over her'. The packed boat stood by and, within a half hour, *Active* had sunk completely.

They then set off in heavy seas and, although favoured by the wind, they suffered waves frequently breaking over them and baling water was constant as they rowed. After rowing for about six hours, they reached Rosslare Harbour pier. There tales of heroism were recounted. In particular they recalled the two firemen, Arthur O'Brien of Byrne's Lane and Patrick Browne of Batt Street, who continued to stoke the furnaces as the water rose around them. They fed coal into the furnaces with their bare hands until the sea water reached their waists. This was done in the full awareness that the cold sea water coming in contact with the boilers could have caused a catastrophic explosion.

11

RELIGION

HOLY WELLS

Every parish in Ireland must, at one time or another, have laid claim to a holy well. These were associated with Christian saints and were often reputed to have healing powers. Some contend that these may have Christianised pagan areas of ancient worship similar to such famous sites as the Oracle of Delphi.

Among the cures reputed to be found in various wells were those for leprosy, insanity, lameness, blindness and infertility. It is said that many of the early Irish monks used the canny idea of settling beside or near the old wells associated with healing properties. By using these wells for baptisms their names became associated with the now 'holy well'. This was done in much the same way as the skilful adaption of early church feast days to make our Christian feasts.

Whitethorn or ash tree shadowing a holy well was regarded as particularly sacred. Ceremonials grew up at these wells. The pilgrim would 'do the stations' by moving three or nine times around the well. The 'proper' way was to move from east to west, following the apparent motion of the sun. Prayers associated with the patron saint were recited. The pilgrim then knelt and bathed hands, forehead and the afflicted part. He or she made the sign of the cross and sometimes sipped the water or even carried some home.

Some became centres of organised pilgrimage and usually commenced on the feast day of the particular saint. As such they sometimes continued for seven days, as at 'Tobar Chriost' in the parish of Ballyoughter, which commenced on St John's Eve. This particular pilgrimage only died out in the 1820s.

Many photos of holy wells show bushes festooned with ribbons, medals and pictures. This came about following a tradition of leaving a strip from the pilgrim's garment or some religious token on the nearby tree or bush.

There are no outright claims that the water in holy wells had any natural medicinal qualities. It was believed that the rituals and prayer in honour of their patron saint effected cures.

Wexford is thought to have had at least 120 venerated wells. Place names are often the only remaining clue to the existence of such wells. There are said to have been wells at Killiane, Killnenor, Kilyshal (Bunclody), Kilnamanagh, Rathangan, Screen, Rathaspeck (locally called 'The Dutchman's'), Taghmon (known as 'the Nunnery'), Enniscorthy (called 'Burn's Well'), and three in Adamstown named as 'Callop's', 'Henry's' and 'John's'.

RELIGION AS GAEILGE

We often forget how prevalent our native language was in County Wexford. In the Visitation Book of Bishop Sweetman, dated 1753, he notes that the confirmation sermons were delivered in Irish in six locations of the county.

It is also noted that Father O'Brien, who ministered in both Bree and Davidstown, was eloquent in his sermons through Irish. O'Brien had a Mass house at Garr. The good priest would later die of head injuries received through falling from his horse. On that occasion he was returning from christening a girl called Rose Whitty. Tradition has it that the child would live to the age of 104 years.

Father Redmond was parish priest of Kilrane but there are reports of him preaching through Irish in Ballyphilip, Rathgarogue and New Ross. Another priest renowned for such preaching was Father James Nolan of New Ross. Likewise, Father Thomas Broaders gave explanations of the sacraments through Irish.

For such preaching to be in demand, the general population of the county must have understood the language.

THE PATTERN

The word pattern comes from the Irish *patrún* or, to use the English version, patron. Most, if not all, Irish parishes had a patron saint. On the saint's feast day, the parishioners celebrated what was known as the patron's day. Just like in Wexford, some older people quite naturally refer to the crescent as the 'chrisnen' or the bridge as the 'brudge', and so the patron day became the Pattern Day.

In the older 'Celtic Catholic Church', before The Reformation and the even more insidious Counter Reformation, the festivities began with religious devotions at the church. This came to an end when the confiscation and destruction of Roman Catholic churches took place in the 1540s and the 1690s. By 1700, the devastation was such that very few churches remained under Catholic control and public religious ceremonies almost disappeared.

The ever-resourceful faithful found alternative ways to celebrate their saint's feast day. While many of the laity paid homage at the saint's shrine or in the ruins of their local church, most devotions took place at the holy well.

The disappearance of Catholic churches and the introduction of Penal Laws made these well gatherings all the more important, especially on the feast day of their patron saint.

Much of this happened without any official clerical direction. Over time the Pattern Days became noted for unorthodox forms of devotion and often-rowdy amusements. The clergy tried to keep matters under control and at the Synod of Tuam in 1660, the following decree was announced: 'Dancing, flute-playing, bands of music, riotous revels and other abuses in visiting wells and other holy places are forbidden ...'

Despite what we often think, Ireland a few centuries ago was not half as clerically influenced as it became in later years. No one paid much attention to that decree or even the Penal Laws of the early eighteenth century which included the infamous 'Act to prevent further Growth of Popery'. This Act had a clause to prohibit 'the riotous and assembling together of many thousands of papists to the said wells and other places', prescribing a fine of 10*s* on all who met at wells and 20*s* on vendors of 'all ale, victuals or other commodities', with a public flogging in default of payment. Enjoined on all magistrates was the demolition of 'all crosses, pictures and inscriptions that are anywhere publickly set up, and are the occasion of any popish superstitions'.

Even this law was ineffective in suppressing Pattern Days because it depended on the local gentry for enforcement and most of the gentry turned a blind eye on what was, for the most part, a harmless local custom. Thus, Pattern Days continued to flourish on into the nineteenth century.

Croker's *Researches in the South of Ireland* gives a description of the revels during a Pattern Day in Gougane Barra, County Cork in 1813 and no doubt Wexford people had just as much fun:

> After having satisfied our mental craving, we felt it necessary to attend to our bodily appetites, and for this purpose adjourned to a tent where some tempting slices of curdy Kerry salmon had attracted our notice. In this tent, with the exception of almost half an hour, we remained located from half-past seven in the evening, until two o'clock the following morning, when we took our departure from Cork. After discussing the merits of this salmon, and washing it down with some of 'Beamish & Crawford's Porter' we whiled away the time by drinking whiskey-punch, observing the dancing to an excellent piper, and listening to the songs and story-telling which were going on about us. As night closed in, the tent became crowded almost to suffocation, and dancing being out of the question, our piper left us for some other.

While the clergy and the Penal Laws failed to suppress Pattern Day celebrations, the Great Famine caused the custom to almost die out. In his book of 1849, *Popular Irish Superstitions*, Sir William Wilde paints a bleak picture of the land and the culture at that time:

> The old forms, and customs too, are becoming obliterated. The festivals are unobserved and the rustic festivities neglected or forgotten – the bowlings, the cakes, the prinkums [a peasant ball], do not often take place when starvation and pestilence stalk over a country, many parts of

which appear as if a destroying army had but recently passed through it.

After the Famine, and during the Victorian era, what was left of the Catholic laity slowly began to regain middle-class status. It was a time when Victorian 'respectability' assumed the sanctity of moral law and many of the old customs were discouraged or forbidden because they offended the sanctimonious. Many Catholics began to borrow the code of acceptable behaviour from their Protestant neighbours; who were largely Puritan and also out of touch with the manners and modes of the country people. Many of the people who survived the Famine chose to put as much distance between themselves and the old ways as they could. Sadly, succeeding generations continued to distance themselves from what was perceived as the old-fashioned ways of a poor, down-trodden and ignorant country and because of this much of the gaiety of traditional rural life was lost.

With the resurgence of interest in all things Irish, the pattern returned but in a much more subdued and official way and they focused more on cemeteries, perhaps because many of the wells were lost to development. In urban areas like Wexford, the day is entirely given over to devotions, prayers and the decoration of graves.

But there is some hope yet that we could see a return to pipers, singers and storytellers. Many parishes combine the pattern with a field day or bottle stall or other fundraising event and who knows how they might develop.

MORE ON RELIGION

The religious practices and ceremonies of the past are often recalled as people hark back to better times.

On 17 December 1830 at 2.15 p.m. Revd Dr Donovan preached the annual charity sermon in the Catholic church of Wexford. This sermon, to which the faithful paid admission, was in aid of 'educating, clothing and apprenticing to useful trades, the Poor Children, 340 male and 250 female, of the Lancastrian and

Nunnery Schools'. Donations from non-attenders should be paid to the preacher, to Very Revd Mr Corrin PP, the Catholic clergy, the treasurer or to news offices. It was pointed out that children were received at the schools without religious distinction.

At that time the usual garb of clergymen consisted of a full suit of black cloth, a coat 'long and broad in the skirts and a waistcoat deep in body and close up to the neck', with knee breeches with silver buckles, black cloth gaiters and boots to the knee. A good horse was a prerequisite.

There were set charges throughout Ireland for various religious duties:

Charge for a house of family	2s 6d
Collection of corn per house	1s 3d
Christmas and Easter Sunday	6d per house
Confessions	6d per family
Marriage	£1 8s 2d
Baptism	3s 4d
Mass to remove a soul from Purgatory	10s
Anointing	1s 1d

The bishop received half a guinea from each marriage and two guineas each for holy oils, dinners and oats for the horse.

12

LOOKING BACK

It is an interesting exercise to look back at the county at random dates in its past to remind ourselves of the changes that may have occurred in the lifestyles and interests of our ancestors over a few decades.

WEXFORD IN 1922

What was Wexford like as the Irish Civil War was being fought? Looking back, it is surprising how many things look the same but at the same time there have been momentous changes.

The biggest thing about Wexford and Ireland in 1922 was, of course, the violence. There was a war going on and the papers were full of reports of deaths and court cases revolving around the Civil War. One casualty was James Roche, a native of King Street, who was one of three civilians stopped by National troops in Passage, County Cork. After shots were fired he was fatally injured. There were reports of a large number of prisoners removed to Dublin from Wexford Military Barracks on the 7.40 train. In the week before Christmas 1922, two armed and masked men entered the offices of the goods store at Wexford's North Station. They held the clerical staff at the point of a revolver and destroyed the telephone apparatus. On leaving they warned the staff to remain for thirty minutes 'under the death penalty' as the newspapers reported it.

But, like in all conflicts, life went on. Trade prospered and entertainment proceeded. Christmas fare, such as Tate's sugar – granulated, cube and castor – was on offer at Godkin's. N. Furlong reminded people to get the 'Xmas Joint' from their shop at the New Market, The Bullring. The Imperial Hotel was selling plum pudding ready for use at 2s 3d for a 1-pound bowl and up to 5s 6d for a 3-pound bowl. They also offered 'biscuits in fancy tins' and Xmas stockings. It seems odd to find a hotel in the retail trade.

The Saint Vincent de Paul Society were appealing for funds to 'supply over a hundred families with Christmas Dinner and coal during the winter'. Also helping the poor was a Pierrot Concert at the Theatre Royal. This was a concert of local talent that even had its own orchestra whose members included the Misses Fitzsimon, Redmond, O'Keefe, Fennell and Murphy on violins with Mr McEvoy playing cello. Master W. Pettit played triangle and N. Kehoe played both flute and piccolo and P. Berry was the drummer. Showstoppers in the programme included 'What a Difference the Navy Made to Me' and 'Whose Baby Are You?'.

In the list of fairs for December the one in Castlebridge was advertised for the 26th, as was Broadway.

Mass in Cleariestown church was enlivened when Mass goers found four men tied to the gates. The newspaper stressed that they were 'not native to the parish'. They had signs that read 'robbers beware' around their necks.

In another war-related piece, there was note of awards from the Shaw Commission from the *Dublin Gazette* for damages to property. Mr Foley of North Main Street was awarded £5,000 for premises and £3,300 for stock burned while J. Merriman of Commercial Quay got £750 for furniture burned. These and other claims arose from 'the burning of Mr E.P. Foley's premises in May 1921 following the wounding of Mr McGovern District Inspector of the RIC'.

There was a complaint at the Wexford District Council of people from Wexford being buried in Drinagh. The caretaker informed the meeting that 'the relatives had no burial rights there'. Mr White was apparently annoyed that 'people were taking French leave with the place'.

Doctor Greene was put 'in complete charge of the County Hospital' and advertising started for a physician for the Fever Hospital who would be consulting physician to the County Hospital and administer anaesthetics at a salary of £200 a year.

Edward O'Rourke of St Peter's Square, who died at the age of 98, was thought to be the oldest inhabitant of the town. He had been 'prominent in the pig trade' and was noted as a member of the Confraternity of the Holy Family.

The recent burning of Wexford Courthouse popped up at the Corporation meeting where James McNally claimed £250 in compensation for losses and his wife claimed a further £150. The Gas Company sought £15 for destruction of a meter in the incident. The mayor stated 'there was a question whether the burning was malicious'.

Such were the concerns of our people as they headed into Christmas ninety years ago.

WEXFORD IN 1946

Ireland in 1946 was still emerging from what we called The Emergency but others called a world war. The LDF had not been disbanded. Rationing was still a way of life. People were still hearing of loved ones killed or injured in the conflict.

Petrol coupons were issued dated up to the end of the year, indicating that the supply was not expected to improve. Supplies had dwindled because of the wet summer and the use of fuel in transporting volunteers into rural areas to help with the harvest.

There were smiles on chocolate lovers' faces with news that supplies were expected – 'the first for some considerable time'.

The price of eggs was fixed by the government to prevent profiteering. Beekeepers were given special permission to purchase up to 10lbs of sugar for winter-feeding. For Castlebridge people going to town meant using the old bridge at Carcur.

What would bring them to Wexford? They might be going to the pictures where the Capitol Cinema was showing, 'by special request', *Rebecca* starring Laurence Olivier. The advertising stated 'this film takes 2 hours to show and will be on screen at 7 o'clock sharp'.

Then there was the shopping. So many of the old shops are now but a memory. Harry Stones were offering Brenner's sausages and puddings. Remember that shop? It was where The Book Centre now stands. It had groceries, meat and a pub. Whelan's in The Bullring offered 'traced linens for embroidery' – anther lost pastime that thrived before television and other distractions. At Corish's Stores on Custom House Quay you might buy an iron bedstead and fibre mattress for about a fiver. Matty Furlong at South Main Street was offering wedding presents.

Sullivan's in The Bullring would sell men's box-calf boots with toe caps and a light sole for only 23*s* or Bison Brand 'stout nailed boots with toe plates and iron heels' for 35*s* 9*d* a pair. In 1946 job offers included, 'A married all round farm worker, must be good ploughman offering free housing, firing, milk and potatoes. Good home to suitable person – wages £30.' So that pair of boots took almost a month's wages.

There was a much more transparent society then – well in some ways. When Michael Cross, a retired locomotive superintendent of Abbey Street died, the list of charitable bequests hit the local papers. These included £300 for Masses for his soul, £500 to the Adoration Convent, £500 to the Mercy Nuns and £500 for the Maynooth Mission to China. He also left £500 to the St Vincent de Paul Society to benefit the poor of Wexford and £250 to the Christian Brother in Wexford as well as £200 to the 'Infirm Clergy Fund of the Diocese of Ferns'.

Among items offered for sale in the small ads were: 'A motor cycle – no back tube, no light, what offer?'; 'Dark bay pony, quiet in harness and traffic – Monck Street'; 'Ferrets – males 30/='. Nicholas Lambert, at 2 North Main Street, was looking to buy crab apples while Michael O'Gorman at Monument House was purchasing blackberries. We also include a selection of ads to bring back memories.

Hassett's remind us of the wet winter that year but also that the idea of lack of sunshine as bad for health is not new. Joyce's show the range of items that were necessary in the Wexford of 1946. L&N was the London & Newcastle stores, reminding us that Ireland was once part of the Empire. The advert refers to the books of stamps collected towards gifts – today there are single offers like holiday discounts, then they had whole catalogues.

13

MISCELLANY

Whenever researching a new publication, hundreds of small items are found that cannot sustain a chapter in their own right are too valuable to be neglected. Here is a selection of these little nuggets of local lore that otherwise might be lost forever.

BALLY BRENNAN SISTERS

In *A Briefe Description of ye Baronie Forthe*, by Sir William Petty about the year 1670, we find the following under the heading 'A Ballybrennan Peece' (*sic*), 'A Chapelle dedicated to the Seven Sisters, at one birth brought forth, at Ballybrennan, commonly called in Irish "Shagh-Eneen Eee", or the "Seven Daughters of Hugh", their father so called, neere to which is a fountain, wherein young languishing infants being bathed, have undeniablie, by the Divine clemency been miraculously restored to perfect health and strength.'

BRIDGE CARRIED AWAY

On the night of 16 January 1867 the bridge at New Ross was carried away by a flood and a flow of ice. The bridge had been built by Lemuel Cox, the man who built the Wexford Oak Bridge in 1796. It was 510ft long and had a portcullis 27ft wide to allow ships through. It earned £800 a year in tolls. After the loss of the bridge a new act was made to replace it. The new bridge opened in August 1869 having cost over £50,000, including £12,334 paid to the owners of the old bridge.

BURIAL OF A SUICIDE

In 1807 Francis Magee, a soldier in the Tyrone Militia stationed at Wexford, committed suicide. His remains were buried at midnight on the site of the Wexford Gasworks near the present Talbot Hotel.

ATTEMPTED MURDER?

Captain Hunt, agent to Sir Hugh Palliser, reported being fired at on his way home from Wexford to Castletown House, Carne, in 1847. It was generally believed at the time that he was not fired at – that some person was fowling near where he was passing. However, Captain Hunt had two policemen to guard him until near his death, which took place a few years later.

CAT'S REVENGE?

George Tuthill, a young lad, 17 years of age, was washed off the rocks east of Hook Tower Lighthouse, in 1861. He was attempting to drown a cat that had killed some pigeons belonging to him, and it was blowing a heavy gale when a wave caught him and carried him away. His body was never found.

CAUTIONARY TALE TO YOUNG CHARISMATIC POLITICIANS

Young Charismatic Politicians should be very wary of visiting Wexford. Michael Collins visited Wexford in April 1922. John F. Kennedy visited in June 1963.

Collins arrived in Wexford by train in the evening and the arrival of his train from Dublin was heralded by the detonation of fog signals, left on the tracks outside town. Kennedy arrived in the GAA Park by helicopter, which attracted great attention.

The next morning, Collins attended eleven o'clock Mass in the Franciscan church and had breakfast with the friars afterwards.

Kennedy is said to have halted his motorcade to chat with some nuns along the way.

Collins visited Pierces and was supposedly pictured with one of the sturdy 'high nelly' bicycles manufactured there. It is reputed that he later ordered a consignment of these bikes for the new Irish Army.

Kennedy spoke in County Wexford about working in a local factory if his ancestors had not left for America.

In later years many stories circulated about Collins' love life and there was speculation about affairs with famous women.

Kennedy was romantically linked with many women including film stars like Marilyn Monroe.

Collins was a young leader who aroused great emotions in Irish people. Kennedy was the youngest American president and an inspiration to many.

Within months of visiting Wexford, Michael Collins was shot by a sniper at Beal na mBlath. Within months of visiting Wexford, John F. Kennedy was assassinated by a sniper in Dallas.

Controversy has surrounded the name of Collins' killer over the decades. Controversy surrounds the JFK assassination to this day.

Be careful all young, charismatic, politicians who visit Wexford.

COTTAGE DANCE

In May 1939 a Mrs Connors of Killabeg Ferns appeared in court charged with permitting her Board of Health cottage to be used for a public dance. In court it was stated that she lived in the cottage with her two children and her lodger with his wife and two children. A number of people attended but she did not charge admission. One lady brought tea, sugar, a loaf, biscuits and sugar. Another brought bread, tea and butter. She provided tea for the crowd. She said she had intended to have a game of cards but did not do it because she was told she needed a licence. She was fined £10.

COURSING CLUB

The first meet for sport of the Hook and Wexford Coursing Club, took place at Dunganstown in 1876.

CROMWELL AT ENNISCORTHY

A little-reported episode of the Cromwellian years is the re-taking of Enniscorthy. It happened in 1651 and we have the words of old Ironsides himself to report it: 'The enemy surprised Enniscorthy in this manner. Some Irish gentlemen feasted the soldiers and sent in women to sell them strong water [whiskey to you and me] of which they drank too much. Then the Irish fell upon them, took the garrison and put all officers and soldiers to the sword.'

DISAPPEARING SHORELINE

Looking out from the quays in Wexford on a clear evening, one can discern the points of The Raven and Rosslare Burrow as they appear to naturally close off Wexford Harbour. The Raven Point is in the parish of Saint Margaret's that most people commonly refer to as Curracloe. It is said that in the century between 1750 and 1850 the sea encroached a distance of 1 mile on that headland. The church of Curracloe was washed away and a castle that stood on the new shoreline was demolished. The castle may have mirrored a Martello Tower that had stood on the Rosslare side of the inlet. That tower also suffered from the power of the encroaching sea. Its base was undermined and eventually the British Board of Works had it removed some time prior to the Famine.

DROWNING

In January 1876 a man named Coghlan drowned in the river Slaney, near Newtownbarry, whilst in pursuit of a pig that he was driving.

FAIRS IN THE EIGHTEENTH CENTURY

In 1747 there were fifty-six fairs held in County Wexford at twenty-five locations. Ferns and New Ross had five, with four each in Gorey, Enniscorthy, Limbrick, Ballycanew, Coolgreaney and Scar. Camolin had three and Bunclody, Moneyhore, Ragory, Mohurry and Ballyhack had two. There was one each in Crosstown, Banogue, Clohamon, Monamolin, Nash, Scarawalsh, Killurin, Kilninor and Our Lady's Island.

Wexford, Taghmon and Castlebridge had no fairs at the time. Most trade was between farmers themselves as dealers and exporters were very scarce.

By 1777 there were twenty-eight locations and sixty-nine fairs. Taghmon had been added. Still, between 8 December and 1 February there were no fairs in the county. This is because the roads were not suitable for herding stock in bad weather.

English farmers were buyers at the time but trade was slow. Communication between the counties was slow and uncertain. There were only a few slow ships carrying cattle to England in the summer of 1777.

FIRST WORKHOUSE BIRTH

The first birth took place in the Enniscorthy Union Workhouse in January 1843. It was that of a female to parents named Quinn.

FRENCH REVOLUTION

During the French Revolution it is said that a member of the County Wexford gentry – a landlord in the New Ross district named Tottenham – ended up in a French prison. On hearing of this, Father Philip Crane went to Paris where Tottenham faced the guillotine.

Disguised as a miller and carrying a flour sack, Crane approached the prison and, at great personal risk, gained access. Inside he changed clothes with Tottenham who then left the gaol in disguise. Father Crane remained in prison but was released later when he could prove his credentials.

Some years later he was guest of honour at a banquet in New Ross hosted by Tottenham. The priest was given a monetary reward and his priory was granted a nominal rent of 10s per annum in recognition of his brave deed.

On his death in 1823 the grave of Father Crane at Saint Mary's became a place of pilgrimage. Clay taken from the grave was believed to have curative powers.

GAS LIGHTING

The town of Enniscorthy was first lit with gas in 1852. A public dinner was held at the Portsmouth Arms Hotel, Enniscorthy, to celebrate.

GREAT FIRE AT THE MEDICAL AND DRUG STORE, SLANEYSTREET, ENNISCORTHY, IN 1874

Not a particle was saved from the house and the proprietor had to escape through a back window into another house.

HA HA RATH

Little do we know where we drive. If you take the road past the church at Rathaspeck, heading for Johnstown Castle, beware because you are travelling over the site of the Ha Ha Rath. At the time of the road building in the late 1800s, the removal of raths was a very serious business. They were thought to be the homes of the faeries and workers were loath to disturb them and bring on their wrath. Tradition tells that as this particular rath did not have a name at the time they decided to christen it with the name offered by the first person to approach. This turned out to be a young lady who could only laugh when asked to christen a rath and so it was called the Ha Ha Rath.

HARE CHASE IN STREET

One evening in March 1952, when Bobby Martin was walking a hound in the Windmill Field in Taghmon, he was surprised to see a hare jump over the wall that bounded the road. The hare, chased by a hound, made of down the High Street.

At the junction of Joseph Street and Main Street it turned and took off up Cinema Road. Then it entered Mr Codd's field and escaped.

HEALTH

We often look back to the past through rose-tinted glasses, seeing golden days, warm nights and long to live in a nostalgic haze. Health is one area where the modern people would get a rude awakening if they travelled back a century or so.

In the *Wexford Herald* of 20 November 1806, persons willing to subscribe to the erection of a Dispensary and Fever Hospital were invited to enter their names on paper at Mr Irvine's Post Office. 'As soon as 100 guineas is raised a committee will be arranged for its establishment.'

Life subscription was 10 guineas or annual subscription was 1 guinea. Patent medicines on offer at that time included:

Aperient Soda Powders – a mild pleasant laxative
 relieving heartburn, bile and nausea
Pectoral Elixir of Hippo and Squills
Dr James Fever Powders
Ching's Worm Lozenges
Butlers Family Pills
Extract of Red Jamaica
 Sarsaparilla for scrufola
Lancaster Blackdrop
 (a preparation of opium)
 for nervous and
 spasmodic diseases.
Bears Grease
ANTI-STIFF –
 an embrocation
 recommended
 for cricketers,
 pedestrians, cyclists,
 hunters, fencers and tourists.

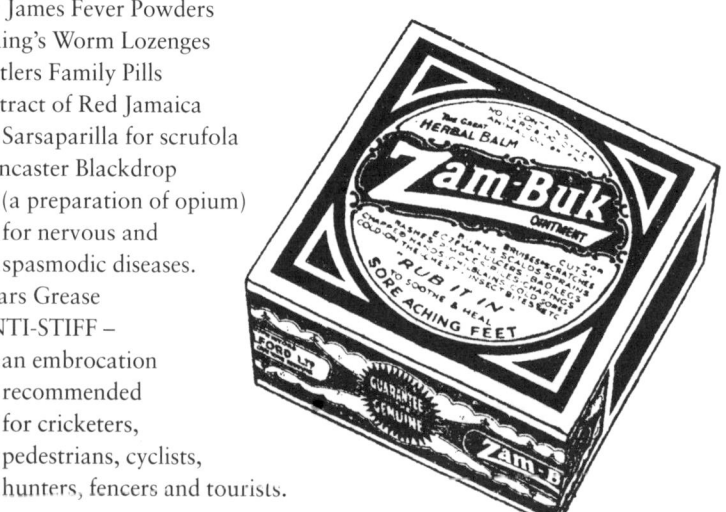

HELPING A SLAVE

In January 1861 Frederick Solly Flood, whose descendants would occupy Ballynaslaney, was in court seeking a writ of habeas corpus to bring John Anderson to England. Anderson was a slave who had escaped from the United States to Canada and the US authorities wanted him returned. Flood's plan was to get him to England from where he could not be taken back.

ILLICIT MALT

A large seizure of illicit malt was made on Forth Mountain by the Wexford Excise Officers in 1836. It was found in a large, new, man-made cave.

INSANITY CAUSES

In the 1901 census, Enniscorthy Lunatic Asylum had 447 patients. The patients were identified by initials only. Almost all were born in County Wexford and the list of each patient included a diagnosis and cause of insanity. Causes of insanity included: religion, excessive smoking, lawsuit, love affair, jealousy, reverse of fortune, pride, effect of foreign climate and drink.

IRON BAR ASSAULT

Peter Murphy, of Ballycanew, died from the blow of an iron bar inflicted by John Sunderland at Finn's public house, Ballycanew, in 1834. Sunderland was transported for life.

LIGHTNING STRIKE

A man named Balfe was killed by lightning whilst ploughing in a field near Carnew in 1844. The horses were also killed.

MEDICAL SOCIETY

A medical society for the county of Wexford was established in 1877, with Dr Goodisson as president and Dr Drapes as hon. secretary and treasurer. The objectives were: to bring together and promote a kindly feeling amongst the members of the profession scattered through the county and, by collective action, to advance the interests of the profession generally, as well as its individual members.

MURDER AND EXECUTION

Anthony Leonard, Esq., was murdered near Annaghs (Kilkenny side), New Ross, in 1833. The murder was perpetrated between two and three o'clock in the afternoon. Mr Leonard resided in New Ross at the time he was murdered. On the day following the murder there was to be an auction of crop and stock seized for £125 rent due to Mr Leonard by one of his tenants. Two brothers were arrested for the murder, and tried at Kilkenny Assizes. They were found guilty and sentenced to be hanged. They were executed on the spot where the murder was perpetrated.

SPRING WATER AT NEW ROSS

In 1885 it was claimed that the sweetest water in all of Ireland was to be found in a spring under the River Barrow at New Ross. This water was found when soundings were being taken for the construction of the bridge between Wexford and Kilkenny in 1876. Cherry Brothers, owners of Creywell Brewery and mineral waters, were in need of a good supply of water and were not slow to harness the new well. They spent $450 piping the water to their premises. Prior to the find, all their water was transported in carts from the upper end of New Ross. Incidentally, this brewery had started out as a distillery owned by Roe and Fletcher in 1784.

NUNS 1889

In September 1889 a number of young ladies left New Ross for Queenstown en route to San Francisco to enter convents there. Among them was Miss Lizzie Murphy of Mount Howard. The twelve girls were in the charge of two nuns including Mother Martin, a sister of James Martin, The Moyne, Enniscorthy. Three of the young ladies were from Wexford town – Julia Lynch, Kate Rossiter and Mary Martin. They were to join the Order of Mercy.

ODD ACCIDENT

In the newspaper of 1917 we find a report of a very unfortunate accident. On the day in question a van owned by the Anglo American Oil Company was crossing what locals now call the Old Bridge at Carcur – long since demolished. In the passenger seat, William Moore of Allen Street was, for some reason, carrying a loaded gun. Without warning the firearm discharged.

Edward Ryan of Temperance Row was walking along the bridge at the time and was hit in the ear and side of the head. He fell to the ground, shouting that he had been shot.

Tim Hanley, the driver, stopped immediately and had the boy taken to the infirmary where Dr Furlong, the house surgeon, treated his injuries. Thankfully these were not life-threatening, which was in itself miraculous considering he was only about 5 yards away from the weapon when it fired. Added to this was how unfortunate an incident it was by virtue of the fact that Ryan and his companion were the only people on the bridge at the time. Because the gun was borrowed only the previous day there was a prosecution under the Defence of the Realm Act.

LIFEBOAT DASH OVER LAND

In 1874 an Italian brig called *Vittorisso G* was wrecked in Bannow Bay. The Duncannon Lifeboat rescued the crew after it had been carried 5 miles over land to be launched.

PIONEERS

The first procession of the Catholic Total Abstinence Society took place in 1877 at Enniscorthy, when upwards of 2,000 teetotallers marched in procession, accompanied by four bands.

PIRATE RAID

On 1 January 1851 the Wexford-based schooner *Sybille*, owned by John Barrington, was boarded and robbed by pirates in the Bospherous.

PRICES

A great favourite when looking back is prices. Who has never chatted about how much they could get for a pound and still have change? One word of caution when reading the following prices – the purchaser did not have had a wage packet even near to yours, so apparent bargains were often relatively expensive. The items on offer also appear quite mysterious in the twenty-first century.

In 1811 coal was 2*s* per cwt; potatoes 3*d* per stone; butter 1*s* 6*d* per pound; whiskey 10*s* per gallon; bacon 8*d* per lb; eggs 8*d* per dozen; milk 3*d* per quart; cheeses 1*s* per pound.

By 1902 tea cost 2*s* per pound; bacon 7*d* per pound; false teeth 11*s* a set; carbide 6*d* per pound; and Pierce bikes set you back 10 guineas.

At the start of the First World War maid's coats cost 10*s*; men's overcoats 32*s* 6*d*; a Ford car five-seater was £135 and a two-seater was £125; a light-weight motorcycle was 25 guineas; and records were 1s 1d each.

As another war started in 1939, Edmond Hassett MPSI (whose telephone was No. 1) offered: peroxide toothpaste, two for 7d; super brillantine two for 1s 4d; kidney pills two for 1s 4d; eye water, two for 1s 4d; liquid soapless shampoo, two for 7d; Ruth Lane perfume, two for 1s 4d; toilet paraffin, two for 1s 7d. As that war came to an end these prices prevailed: tea 4s per pound; sugar 6d per pound; butter 2s 4d per pound; lard 1s 2d per pound; coffee 3s; sausages 1s 3d; and ham 4s 8d.

To start the 'Swinging Sixties', drink and entertainment set you back as follows: bottle of stout 11*d*; large bottle 1*s* 7*d*; whiskey 4*s* 4*d* a glass; lager 1*s* 6*d* a pint; dancing to the Majestic Showband 5*s*.

RAILWAY ARRIVES

The first sod turned for a railway in this county was at Poulmounty in January 1856.

ROBBERY

A man named Alexander Roche was arrested whilst attempting to rob the house of Mr Floyd, Artramont, in 1833. The servant girl, hearing a noise, went upstairs to see what caused it. When she observed Roche in one of the rooms she immediately locked the door and ran for assistance.

ST PATRICK'S DAY, 1777

In Enniscorthy, on St Patrick's Day, 1777, an aged clergyman called Father Wickham, who lived in Templeshannon, was walking out on the evening of St Patrick's Day when he met a man of the town who was very much under the influence of drink. He went to remonstrate with him about his state. It is not known whether the drunken man struck the clergyman or simply staggered under the influence and fell against him but Father Wickham fell and one of his legs was broken. The old gentleman was carried home, put to bed, and 'never again rose from it, but died after suffering much pain'.

SHIP PLUNDERED

The Mayor of Limerick complained to Lord Deputy Bellyngham in 1549, that a ship belonging to the Port of Limerick, on her voyage from Spain to that city with a cargo of wine, was wrecked on the Wexford coast and plundered by the inhabitants.

SHIPWRECK

The ship *Columbia*, bound from New Orleans to Liverpool, was wrecked near the Hook Lighthouse in 1852. She had a cargo of 3,800 bales of cotton, and 5,000 bushels of Indian corn. Eleven of the crew were drowned and nineteen saved.

TWO SHIPWRECKS IN ONE DAY

The ship *Hottingeur*, bound from Liverpool to New York, was wrecked on Blackwater Bank in 1850. That same day the Russian brig *Geisler Adolph*, travelling from Koningsberg to Liverpool, was wrecked at Ballygeary. In both cases the crews were saved by the praiseworthy exertions of the country people.

SLANEY NAVIGATION

A public meeting was held at Enniscorthy to consider the advisability of improving the navigation of the River Slaney between that town and Wexford in 1832. Lord Carew, lieutenant of the county, presided. Mr Yignoles CE attended and explained that it would cost £33,000 to make a canal from Pouldarrig to Brownswood, and from thence to use the river. The average annual traffic on the river at that time between Wexford and Enniscorthy was 56,000 tons.

STREET NAMES

The names of streets are a constant source of fascination. While it would take a full book and more to recount all such names we will look here at a small but interesting sample from around the county. One great fact about the old names, before we started the process of using just patriotic names (or more sadly, in recent times, weird concoctions of descriptive and pop culture), was the way street names reminded us of our history. Wexford town had Petticoat Lane and Garment Lane but both locations are lost with the folk memory. Cockpit Lane was well known in New Ross. It led from the top of Mary Street towards Irishtown. This would suggest that the old sport of cock fighting once thrived in that locality with a cock pit located there. Houses were later built up along the route and it became Houghton Place. In Gorey there was the lyrically named Shoeover Street. This was changed to Grattan Street. The oldest name for a street in Enniscorthy is believed to be Templeshannon.

SUFFOCATED

Two women, named Finn and Roche, suffocated in bed in Ballytarsna in 1868. The night being cold, the women brought a fire in a pot into their small bedroom, and were thus suffocated.

TARRING AND SANDING

Two young men were convicted before the magistrates at Duncormack Petty Sessions for tarring and sanding a young woman in 1870

TOWELS FROM 1854

In a newspaper article in 1952 it was reported that Bridget Sinnott of Churchtown, Tacumshane, had in her possession two linen handtowels that had been woven by her grandfather, Thomas Dougan of the Bog, Mayglass, in 1854. He had been one of the last survivors of the famous weavers of Mulrankin. One of the last spinning wheels and looms of the district had been lately presented to the National Museum.

TOWER FALLS

The tower of Adamstown Chapel fell in 1872. Happily there was no injury to life or property.

TREE PLANTING

In 1793 a premium of £5 8s was granted by the Dublin Society to William Webster, a resident in the County Wexford, for having planted 23,390 forest trees during the previous two years.

VAGRANTS

In 1654 the governors of Carlow, Kilkenny, Clonmel, Wexford, Ross and Waterford issued an order. It stated that all wanderers, men and women, and such other Irish within the area, were to be arrested and handed up to Captain Thomas Morgan, Dudley North and John Johnson. If they could not prove that they could maintain themselves then they were to be transported to the West Indies.

VANDALS

Vandalism is not new. In 1859 there were reports of the Christian Brothers School and that of the Presentation nuns in Enniscorthy being broken into. Windows were broken and books wantonly destroyed and a small sum of money was taken. Some things never change.

WORKHOUSE ARSON

Sarah Heffernan and Mary Kehoe, two pauper inmates, set fire to their beds in the Enniscorthy Workhouse, with the intention of destroying the building, in 1866. They were tried at the ensuing Wexford Assizes, found guilty, and sentenced to five years' penal servitude.

BIBLIOGRAPHY

BOOKS

Basset, George, *Wexford County Guide and Directory* (Dublin 1885)
Centenary Record (1958)
Colfer, B. , *Wexford, a Town and its Landscape* (Cork University Press, 2008)
Griffith, G., *Chronicles of County Wexford* (Enniscorthy, 1877)
Hore, P.H., *History of Town and County of Wexford* (1906; reprinted by Professional Books, 1979)
Lacy, T., *Sights and Scenes in Our Fatherland* (Simpkin, Marshall & Company, 1863)
Leach, Nicholas, *Lifeboats of Rosslare Harbour and Wexford* (Nonsuch, 2007)
Ranson, J., *Songs of the Wexford Coast* (Norwood, 1975)
Roche, Rossiter, Hurley & Hayes, *Walk Wexford Ways* (privately published, 1988)
Rossiter, Hurley, Roche & Hayes, *A Wexford Miscellany* (WHP, 1994)
Rossiter, N., *Wexford Port* (WCTU, 1989)
Rossiter, N., *My Wexford* (Nonsuch, 2006)
Rossiter, N., *Wexford, a History, a Tour, a Miscellany* (Nonsuch, 2005)
Rowe, David & Wilson, Christopher (eds), *High Sky – Low Lands* (Duffrey Press, 1996)
Ronan, Gerard, *The Irish Zorro* (Brandon, 2004)
Walsh, Dermot, *Tragedy at Tuskar* (Mercier Press, 1983)

NEWSPAPERS

Wexford Echo   *Wexford Independent*
Wexford Herald   *Wexford People*

JOURNALS

Wexford Historical Society – various articles
The Past – various articles

PERSONAL NOTES/ UNPUBLISHED RESEARCH

Rossiter Nicky – Encyclopaedia of Wexford – unpublished

If you enjoyed this book, you may also be interested in...

Wexford Folk Tales
BRENDAN NOLAN

Wexford has a rich heritage of myths and legends which is uniquely captured in this collection of traditional tales from across the county. Discover the remarkable stories of the 140-year-old man who died a premature death, the arrival of the antichrists (six of them) in Wexford, the dangers of love potions and how two people came back from the dead, together with tales of lurechan mischief, mermaids, grave robbing and buried treasure.

978 1 84588 766 7

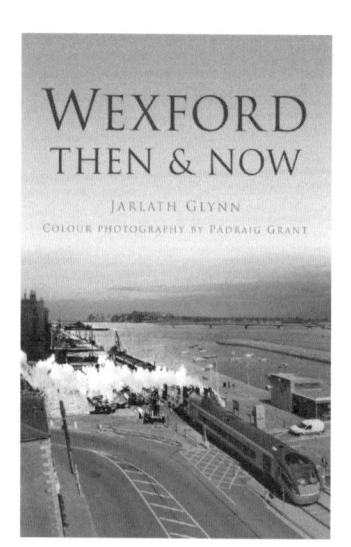

Wexford Then & Now
JARLATH GLYNN

Wexford is a town of great character and individuality. It has been in existence for 1,000 years, and this new publication, researched and written by Jarlath Glynn, explores that vibrant history. This is done through contrasting forty-five archive images with full modern photographs taken by Pádraig Grant. This book will be of great interest to all who know the town as well as providing a vital record of the changing face of Wexford.

978 1 84588 805 3

Visit our websites and discover thousands of other History Press books.

www.thehistorypress.ie
www.thehistorypress.co.uk

The History Press Ireland